MASTERING IN-HOUSE SEO

BLEEDING EDGE STRATEGIES AND TACTICS FROM LEADING IN-HOUSE SEO EXPERTS

PUBLISHED AND COMPILED BY

SIMON SCHNIEDERS

CEO OF BLUE ARRAY

Mastering In-House SEO - Bleeding Edge Strategies And Tactics From Leading In-House SEO Experts

ISBN 9798639691508

© Blue Array - Blue Array Ltd., Reading Bridge House, George Street, Reading Bridge, Reading, Berkshire, RG1 8LS

Published in March 2020

This book is dedicated
to my wife Lacy
and our daughter Amelia.

Simon Schnieders

PRAISE FOR MASTERING IN-HOUSE SEO

Navigating internal politics and processes is one of the greatest challenges in-house SEOs face; a bigger challenge than the SEO discipline itself. This book is packed with wins and solid advice that my younger self would have begged for.

LUKE CARTHY
eCommerce Growth Consultant

A book that achieves the rare feat of going broad and going deep.

ORIT MUTZNIK
Head of SEO at SilkFred

As someone who has been on both sides (agency and in-house), I'm confident both groups will learn a lot about the world of in-house SEO by reading this book.

RICHARD NAZAREWICZ
Technical SEO Manager at the Wall Street Journal

This book is exactly the type of resource I would have loved to have when starting out a decade ago.

KERSTIN REICHERT
SEO Digital Marketing Manager at Tide

If you are an in-house SEO, this book should always be an arm's length away. With case studies, tips and guides, it has everything you need.

ELI SCHWARTZ
Former Director of Growth and SEO at SurveyMonkey

From philosophy to tactics, from technical deep dives to challenging people issues, this book has it all.

DOMINIK SCHWARZ
Chief Inbound Officer at HomeToGo

Covering a lot of ground from case studies to career advice, this book is a tour de force through in-house SEO.

ADAM WHITTLES
Head of SEO at AutoTrader

Simon and the team at Blue Array have created an indispensable guide for future generations of in-house SEO managers.

EMIRHAN YASDIMAN
Technical SEO Lead at Metro Markets

CONTENTS

14 FOREWORD
SIMON SCHNIEDERS | BLUE ARRAY

---

18 HOW I BUILT A COMMUNITY FOR WOMEN TO SUPPORT ONE ANOTHER
AREEJ ABUALI | SEO MANAGER, ZOOPLA

From 1-1 mentoring to running a conference with 250 participants in less then a year. How Women in Tech SEO was founded and grew to an important community in the London Tech scene.

**24 A CULTURE OF AUTONOMY:
BUILDING AN SEO TEAM THAT CAN DO IT ALL**
FABRIZIO BALLARINI | ORGANIC GROWTH & SEO, TRANSFERWISE

Transferwise is the rare case of a company that provides individual teams staggering levels of organisational autonomy. This has allowed Fabrizio, through merit and perseverance, to build an SEO team of 30+ people, with impressive results.

**30 HOW A "SIMPLE" POINT OF VIEW
MADE A £30,000/DAY DIFFERENCE**
LUKE CARTHY | ECOMMERCE GROWTH CONSULTANT

Occasional calls to customer service about checkout problems went unresolved for over a year at this niche ecommerce company. Conventional wisdom was that the company's non web-savvy audience was making mistakes. Until Luke looked at the error log files. And yes, this has a lot to do with SEO.

36 BEYOND TACTICS: PRINCIPLES TO DRIVE STRATEGIC SEO
SIMON DANCE | SVP GROWTH, LYST.COM

There is no shortage of tactics you can use in SEO. But are they what you should focus on? Simon approaches SEO from a principle-based view, and discusses five ways you can rethink SEO from a different perspective.

42 HOW A BEST-PRACTICE GUIDEBOOK HAS HELPED THE TIMES AND THE SUNDAY TIMES TO SUCCEED WITH SEO
ALICE FOSTER | SEO EDITOR, THE TIMES & THE SUNDAY TIMES

When Google changed its policy for news sites using paywalls, the Times wanted to jump at the opportunity to change their approach to SEO. But how to kickstart SEO in a culture where it had been low priority? For Alice, an SEO guidebook was the answer.

46 HOW TO WIN FRIENDS AND INFLUENCE PEOPLE: SEO EDITION
DAVID GERRARD | TEAM LEAD SEO, HEYCAR

The most important ingredient to your success as an in-house SEO is relationship building. But what specifically does that mean? David Gerrard who defected from the agency world into an in-house role, breaks it down in detail.

52 NECESSARY EVIL TO NOTABLE EDGE: OPTIMISING FILTER PAGES FOR RANKING AND CONVERSION
ALINA GHOST | SEO MANAGER, AMARA

When it comes to filter pages, most e-commerce sites just block them from being indexed. But Alina and her team found a way to turn these pages into another source of revenue for her company's online store.

58 REDUCING RISK WITH AUTOMATED SEO TESTING
BEN JOHNSON | FREELANCE SEO CONSULTANT

First, Ben was having sleepless nights before each new tech release, worried it would break something SEO-related. So he built a QA tool that automated crawls. And lo and behold - this tool became a profitable business in itself.

64 DATA-LED JOURNALISM: HOW WE CREATED PAGES MORE PEOPLE WANTED TO READ
JONATHAN JONES | FORMER ORGANIC PERFORMANCE LEAD, MONEYSUPERMARKET GROUP

Shifting away from link building as the primary source of inbound traffic, Jonathan decided he wanted to create better content. And so he dug into the data to uncover what MoneySuperMarket's audience wanted to read about. Here is the tale of this transition.

70 THE PENGUIN PROGNOSTICATOR: GOING AGAINST THE CROWD
ANTONIS KONSTANTINIDIS | HEAD OF SEO, EF ENGLISH LIVE

In 2012, Antonis's company happily used the usual grey-hat ranking techniques, which at the time still worked like a charm. But Antonis needed to convince everyone to abandon what worked - he saw the Penguin's flipper-writing on the wall. Here's how he did it.

76 THINK LAND GRAB: CAREER ADVICE FOR SEOS AND THEIR EMPLOYERS
NEIL MIDDLEMASS | FOUNDER, ASSEMBL

SEO is a digital discipline unlike others, and recruiting for it has unique complexities. Neil offers advice for both SEOs and businesses looking to hire, covering issues like evaluating good fit, why SEOs should land grab, and how companies can handle availability gaps.

82 THE OVERKILL APPROACH TO SCORING YOUR DREAM SEO ROLE
ORIT MUTZNIK | HEAD OF SEO, SILKFRED

Orit recalls how she got her dream SEO role in her dream location. Her recommendations: Burst through the door, use the element of surprise, and outwork everyone else. Yes - all of that as part of your job application.

88 THE SURVIVALIST'S GUIDE TO THE ENTERPRISE SEO JUNGLE
RICHARD NAZAREWICZ | TECHNICAL SEO MANAGER, THE WALL STREET JOURNAL

Coming from small and mid-sized companies, Richard joined the Wall Street Journal in 2018 to lead their SEO. Here is his recipe for success in a corporate environment.

98 PROXIES, PRERENDERING AND PR: LESSONS FROM A BRIEF BRAND CAMPAIGN
JAMIE PEACH | HEAD OF SEO EUROPE, SAMSUNG

Sometimes, things are not in your favour. Jamie talks about the lessons his team took away from supporting a brand campaign with considerable technical challenges... and one other unexpected problem.

104 THE FAST AND FURIOUS: LIFE AS AN SEO EXPERT IN A START-UP
KERSTIN REICHERT | SEO DIGITAL MARKETING MANAGER, TIDE

On the joys and constraints on being the first in-house SEO person in a fast-growing FinTech scaleup - Kerstin recaps her first months at Tide, and what she learned along the way.

112 THE JOURNEY: WHAT TO FOCUS ON AS YOUR CAREER UNFOLDS
SAM ROBSON | DIRECTOR OF AUDIENCE, FUTURE

As the cliché suggests, each career is a journey. And as it evolves, so do you and the things you focus on. Sam looks at three stages of a career, and what he did at each stage that helped him build a career that took him to the top of SEO - and beyond.

118 COLLABORATION AND COORDINATION: AN SEO MASTER LIST TO GET MORE DONE
RIC RODRIGUEZ | SEO CONSULTANT, YEXT

A common feature of how SEO work gets done is in-house teams jostling for developer attention to get things done. Ric has managed to break the mold through a unique, far more collaborative process that leaves everyone better off.

126 HISTORY AND LEGACY: JOINING A COMPANY AS THE FIRST IN-HOUSE SEO
ANGIE ROONEY | SEO PRODUCT LEAD, FINDMYPAST

When Angie joined Findmypast as the first in-house SEO, she had to tread carefully. Past mistakes and wasted efforts meant she had to be as diplomatic as she possibly could. A tale of balancing the need to dig into the past with a steadfast view on the future.

134 SELLING SEO: HOW TO GET A BIGGER BUDGET TO GROW ORGANIC AND YOUR CAREER
ELI SCHWARTZ | FORMER DIRECTOR OF GROWTH AND SEO, SURVEYMONKEY

In his first week at Surveymonkey, Eli made an SEO recommendation one of the chief officers labelled as "the stupidest idea I ever heard." This moment has taught Eli a lesson.

140 WHY SEO IS MORE THAN SEO
DOMINIK SCHWARZ | CHIEF INBOUND OFFICER, HOMETOGO

In this philosophical piece, Dominik takes a critical look at the most common misconceptions around SEO and puts them to the test. He tops it off with his SEO Manifesto.

---

146 IMPOSTER SYNDROME AND SEO: BEATING BACK SPECTERS OF SELF-DOUBT
TRISTRAM DE SILVA | TECHNICAL SEO MANAGER, TICKETMASTER

Imposter syndrome can claw at the confidence of even the most experienced SEO. Tristram recounts his encounters with imposter syndrome and the measures he took to beat it back.

---

156 LIFE IN THE NEWSROOM: SEO IN THE "BREAKING NEWS" LANDSCAPE
CARLY STEVEN | HEAD OF SEO (THE SUN), NEWS UK

Life in a newsroom is different. You deal with a crowd of hardened reporters and editors, respond to breaking news, and aim to rank outside organic results. Carly talks through her experience working in SEO for the Daily Mail and The Sun, along with some of her most important discoveries.

---

162 THE NEED FOR SPEED: SIMPLE PAGE SPEED OPTIMISATIONS TO MAKE YOUR SITE FASTER
ROXANA STINGU | HEAD OF SEO, ALAMY

Getting reports is the easy part - far more difficult is to know what to do when a report tells you that JS rendering is slowing the site down. Roxana shares a primer on what to actually DO to increase page loading times.

170 — SCIENTIFIC SEO: A TEST-DRIVEN APPROACH TO VALIDATING SEO
FELIX WELCKENBACH | FREELANCE SEO CONSULTANT

A/B testing is not well-known in the SEO industry. Yet, it is a powerful method SEOs can use to validate, measure and quantify their ideas and initiatives with. Felix goes through the core concepts you need to know around this type of testing.

176 — THE SEO SCALE: HOW TO TELL IF YOUR NEXT COMPANY MEASURES UP
ADAM WHITTLES | HEAD OF SEO, AUTO TRADER

Making the jump from agency to in-house can be daunting. Which organisations will offer the best opportunities and provide the most support? Adam talks about a scale you can use to measure whether a business stacks up when it comes to investing in SEO.

182 — CROSS-CACHE: WHEN PAGES "JUMPED" COUNTRIES (AND HOW I FIXED IT)
EMIRHAN YASDIMAN | TECHNICAL SEO LEAD, METRO MARKETS

Google stopped ingesting the site maps of this travel aggregator site. At the bottom of the problem lay a complex web of hreflang and noindex tagging - a tricky technical issue that no agency would tackle. By running a manual test and subsequently rolling it out across the site, Emirhan shows how important it is to have an in-house SEO team.

189 — BONUS CONTRIBUTION
WHY YOUR SEO RECOMMENDATIONS DON'T GET IMPLEMENTED (AND WHAT TO DO ABOUT IT)
BEN HOWE | SEO MANAGER, BLUE ARRAY

FOREWORD

When we shared with the SEO world that we wanted to write a book for and about in-house professionals, some of the reactions were sceptical. Many were mentally jarred by the idea of the CEO at the UK's largest SEO agency creating a book about in-house SEO. They thought these were two completely separate worlds, with very different types of people, incentives and models of working.

That is a relatively common perception, no doubt fuelled by the high visibility many agencies and freelancers achieve on social media and in popular publications: Here, the agency experts and freelancers, the thought leaders, armed with expertise from the bleeding edges of SEO, who swoop in to impart a range of best-practice recommendations. Alternatively, we are offered their own interpretation (or misinterpretation) of direction from Google on its inner workings.

The in-house SEO expert, in contrast, is sometimes perceived to be the meek, unassuming character puttering about their obscure craft on the periphery of the marketing team, obediently implementing this imparted wisdom from the thought leaders of our industry.

This image is wrong on at least three levels.

First of all, in-house experts are anything but unassuming fading flowers. Yes, they don't seek the limelight as their agency or freelance counterparts often do, but their work requires them to be supremely proactive. Charisma is in ample supply as well, coming in handy when you need to win over others to do things for you when you don't have formal authority over them.

Second, many agencies' assumed bleeding edge market knowledge is not always what it's chalked up to be. Often, it's the in-house teams who have the time and freedom to really go deep on a specific topic.

Third, just like the world-famous tagline "What happens in Vegas, stays in Vegas", a lot of "What happens in-house, stays in-house". A competitive advantage is best placed outside of industry knowledge and often remains locked within the company or in-house SEO practitioner.

This division — agencies and freelancers here, in-house experts there — is much less stark than commonly perceived. In fact, it's a very mutualistic relationship: Agencies are a good sounding board for in-house teams because of their exposure to multiple clients and industries, and they are perfectly positioned to be both strategic and available tactically when the in-house teams need more hands on deck, as they often do.

It is this symbiotic relationship that, I believe, lies at the very heart of Blue Array's success.

My own in-house experience across names such as Zoopla, Yell and Mail Online had been deliberately directed so I could start and run an agency. I never took a role that wouldn't serve that end goal.

Had I not had my years of in-house insight, I don't believe Blue Array would ever be as wildly successful as it has been. The incredible team I'm blessed to lead has certainly been pivotal, though the in-house understanding gave us that edge.

The book you are holding in your hands opens the kimono on working in-house, and it's meant to be valuable for both agency owners and employees.

For agency owners and freelancers, it serves to understand the struggles in-house people have, and therefore to help run better agencies.

Current and aspiring in-house SEO professionals hopefully benefit from reading fascinating case studies, learning new ways to influence people, and getting inspiration for crafting their careers. Most importantly, they will find that they are not alone in their thoughts and feelings. We all struggle with the same challenges, but mastery is revealed within the book for the wise reader willing to learn from others.

I am beyond excited to share this book with the agency, freelancer and in-house SEO community and everyone who wants to join any one of them.

If Blue Array seems attractive to you as an agency, we're always hiring!

When we started reaching out to the co-authors of this book, one of them said "This is a book I wish I had read when I was starting out".

Well, here it is. May it serve its purpose to educate, captivate, and maybe even commiserate.

Simon Schnieders
Chief Executive Officer at Blue Array
simon@bluearray.co.uk

If you'd like to learn the "Blue Array way" of doing SEO, I invite you to visit www.bluearrayacademy.com

HOW I BUILT A COMMUNITY FOR WOMEN TO SUPPORT ONE ANOTHER

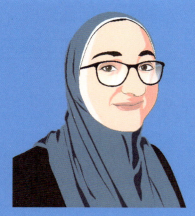

AREEJ ABUALI
SEO MANAGER AT ZOOPLA & FOUNDER OF 'WOMEN IN TECH SEO'

Areej has 6+ years of blended experience in digital marketing, technical SEO, data analysis, account management and web analytics. In 2019 started Women in Tech SEO, a community that has grown to almost a thousand members within only 9 months and culminated in a conference. Areej is a speaker at MozCon, BrightonSEO and Blue Array's LondonSEOMeetup. She holds a BSc in Computer Engineering and an MBA in Information Technology.

Being an in-house SEO can be a pretty lonely job.

But not only that.

It's also that SEO is broad but highly technical, often comes without much formal authority, and requires mastering delicate interpersonal dynamics.

All of that means that there's always way more questions than answers.

THE SEED THAT STARTED THE COMMUNITY

I felt this keenly when in May 2019, I began mentoring women who had just started in new roles in technical SEO and needed someone with an outside perspective.

After around five years in the industry, I had the strong urge to give back and help women who, in my experience, often felt overwhelmed in a largely male work environment and often underestimated their abilities.

Many of the women I spoke to had lots of work experience, but were worried that they were not good enough, that they had knowledge gaps especially in technical matters.

And so I decided to start a support group and community to accomplish four goals:

- Provide a safe space where worries and fears could be aired without fear of judgment
- Create a forum to learn
- Highlight opportunities by posting open positions in the SEO job market
- Elevate freelancers and make them more visible to the industry

A FAST TRAJECTORY

Within a week, the Facebook group had over 100 members, which was a big surprise to me. And thinking that there should be more to it than an online group, I started running monthly meetups in London.

On the first Thursday of the month, around 60 of us get together at a central London location after work, and enjoy up to three talks on topics ranging from technical topics, as well as more general, empowerment-type subjects. Towards the end, there's time for networking, drinks and nibbles.

Things grew very fast - We're now over 900 on Facebook and our meetup speaking slots are booked out until the end of the year.

In August 2019, I decided to take it one big step further and launch a full-scale conference in honour of International Womens' Day.

At the time of writing, I'm applying the last touches to our first conference, very excited to be welcoming 250 delegates from all around the world for a full day of celebrating Women in Tech SEO.

LESSONS LEARNED FROM STARTING A TRIBE

The rapid success of Women in Tech SEO has taught me a few good lessons on how to build a community.

You actually may not need to start a community

I know, this sounds strange at this point. What I mean to say is to look if there is already a community in your area. You don't need to reinvent the wheel. Instead, if you want to contribute to your tribe, ask the organiser of an existing community if they need help. I sure could have used a pair of hands in the early days, but... see the next point.

You don't need to do everything yourself

That's a big lesson learned for me and one I should have heeded earlier on.

But I understand that the earlier I become comfortable with this, the better. There are so many people out there who are willing to help with organising a tribe and building a community, it's neither practical nor conducive to my own sanity to try to control everything myself.

Open up multiple channels

We have the Facebook community, we have the in-person meetups, and I have also started a Slack group which has by now sprouted a healthy bunch of channels.

Not only does branching out a bit help with being more inclusive (hint: not everyone likes Facebook - or Slack), but it also leverages each platform's strengths.

Online & Offline —> 1+1=3

It's almost needless to say that there should always be a physical component to a community. Keeping things online is just too sterile, and the best relationships are built in direct 1-1 conversations.

But at the same time, the online community is absolutely vital to keep things going in between meetups.

I believe that it's this combination of online and offline, as well as the supportive, non-judgmental character of this group that makes Women in Tech SEO unique. There is no way I could have sold 250 conference tickets if it weren't for the strong community character of the group.

Encourage first-time presenters

I received lots of positive feedback on my decision to empower first time speakers to present. Many of our presenters are first-time public speakers, and many times, their presentations are extremely informative.

Our speaker registration is a Google Form that anyone can access. And because of this Open-Door policy I instituted, our speaking slots are booked up until the end of 2020.

Leverage the community for meeting space

The beauty of a work-related community is that many members are able to provide office space. Not only that, we were always able to secure hosting support in the form of drinks and nibbles, which made the experience even nicer.

CONCLUSION

For me, Women in Tech SEO is a dream come true. I would have have never expected it would get this big this fast. And I am incredibly grateful to everyone who has accompanied me on this journey and provided vital support along the way.

If you want to become involved, go to womenintechseo.com, and we'll take it from there!

A CULTURE OF AUTONOMY: BUILDING AN SEO TEAM THAT CAN DO IT ALL

FABRIZIO BALLARINI

ORGANIC GROWTH AND SEO, TRANSFERWISE

Fabrizio began his professional career in SEO and has been in the industry for seven years. After starting as an SEO Specialist, he worked at Ogilvy & Mather UK before joining TransferWise as Head of Organic Growth & SEO in 2015. Fabrizio is also active at conferences, speaking at events such as Turing Fest and Search Leeds.

Joining TransferWise was a leap of faith. I had watched a video from the VP of Growth that talked about how the company worked. I remember thinking if that was how they handled SEO, it would be a great opportunity.

When I arrived, I was introduced to a new way of working and a new culture.

A CULTURE OF AUTONOMY

At the time I started, there were around a dozen teams at TransferWise, all operating independently. Today, that number is closer to 50+ satellite teams, and they still work and organise in a similar way.

"Autonomous" does not mean 100% independent. We still have centralised financial constraints as an organisation, like any big company. But for investment, decision-making, planning and any other operational aspect, the team controls its fate.

In other words, we are not managed by a central planner who dictates our actions or budget. The SEO team has the ability to decide what we do, how much we do at any given time, and how much money we need to do it.

This autonomy also means we don't share resources with other teams. We have everything we need in-team: analysts, designers, content writers and developers. All up, there are about 30 people in the SEO team (a far cry from when I started, which was just me and three developers). This self-

A BIG RISK?

One of the big risks with teams working on their own priorities is that a team can stray in a direction not in line with the larger company strategy. And there have been occasional challenges with this model at TransferWise.

For example, teams have failed with projects or been over-ambitious. Sometimes, two teams have built similar pages or tools. But while this occurs, the benefits of autonomous operation far outweigh the risks or occasional setbacks.

reliance is important, as we don't need to ask for help or sell a project to other teams. If we decide an initiative has value, we implement it. This also allows us to move more quickly, as if we were a small company instead of the $3.5bn organisation we are today.

A SECOND KEY PRINCIPLE

Autonomy is the concept TransferWise's team structure themselves around, but there is another important principle at play: co-ownership. No matter which part of the website is owned by a particular team, another team — so long as they have a specific purpose — can make changes to it.

A recent example was the ongoing effort behind one of our price comparison tools. This is functionality everybody in the industry has struggled with, so we built our own tool from the ground up. It's now grown to the point where it has a dedicated team and engineers. However, parts of the tool are important for SEO, and because our KPI is to increase acquisition across TransferWise, that is where we step in.

The SEO team contributes engineers and resources to maintain and improve the price comparison tool. Just this quarter, our team shipped a number of changes that included new templates and new pages for the tool, without relying on resources of the team who owns it. This is a typical display of the autonomy and co-ownership individual teams enjoy.

THE ROI OF AN AUTONOMOUS TEAM

Having been with the SEO team from the early days, I have seen how we evaluate and measure ROI change as we have grown.

When we first started on the blog, there was almost zero traffic. Our efforts were small scale, with five to ten articles each month. This brought a modest return: traffic rose to 20,000 visitors a month. But for the first six months, we weren't sure what return to expect or if we had under or over-invested in the blog. The important aspect was — as in any culture of autonomy — that we had trust that our work would ultimately pay for itself.

These days, our blog gets over 1 million readers every month and we publish 300+ articles in 15 languages each quarter. More significantly, we have plenty of data to better evaluate the pay-off, whether it happens over a 10, 12 or even 24 month period.

The blog is just one example. Our website only had 15,000 visitors a month during that early period, which wasn't paying back the investment sunk into it. Thanks to the same trust (and our work), volumes have since soared to a few million unique visitors a month.

These kinds of estimates are more difficult to do on the engineering side,

THE ROAD TO REVENUE

The SEO team wasn't focused on ROI early on, but we made moves to position us to generate (and measure) revenue for the company. These were three broad steps we took to achieve this.

1. Find the real numbers

One of the first things I did was to invest time into analytics, so we could be confident attributing visitors to SEO and not other marketing measures. Taking a hard attitude on numbers didn't paint me in a great light during those first few quarters, but I thought it better to convey an accurate picture rather than pretend everything was fine.

2. Ship stuff

There wasn't any big secret to prove ourselves beyond showing we could get things done. Whether that meant writing a blog post or building a calculator tool, we got in and did it. However, like most things in SEO, it takes time to start ranking and to get a feel for whether you are on the right track.

3. Don't make revenue the target

Revenue was not our first KPI, but indexed pages. That was a basic measure of our productivity. Back then, we only had 2,000 odd pages compared to the millions we have today. Of course, those pages weren't the end goal. We wanted pages attracting clicks, so clicks became the next KPI over the next six to nine months.

When you get that right, traffic is a natural consequence, and revenue flows as a result. But we needed to start by focusing on building out the site and bringing in traffic in before we could start to measure success by revenue.

but for content, we very much focus on forecasts. We know how much money each article we produce generates, and can forecast what the costs and ROI on writing about a particular topic are likely to be.

Today, the SEO team delivers an overall return that more than pays for itself. We have the cheapest acquisition channel in the company, measuring ROI on every project across a 12-month period. At the moment, we enjoy a particularly high ROI on much of what we ship, with a break-even period of just two to three months.

MOVING BEYOND THE TEAM

Businesses like Spotify or Skyscanner use guilds in a more committed way, but we do apply the concept and get some benefit.

(For those unfamiliar with a "guild", it is a group of people who work across different teams but meet to discuss and share knowledge around a specific skill or interest, like engineering.)

TransferWise has grown dramatically over the past few years, and our autonomous team culture meant specialists weren't meeting enough to solve bigger challenges. With hundreds of engineers in the company, it made sense to bring them together with an engineering guild.

This is also the case with SEO. We have SEOs across three to four teams who deal with organic traffic. We are reaching the point where SEO is more than a team, but a guild of people with a certain skill. For example, the editorial team has one or two SEOs. The product engineering team does too, since they deal with landing pages and the CMS.

Training this group as a team, even though they don't report or work with each other, will happen sooner rather than later. Looking to the future, we may also introduce someone to help manage more cross-team initiatives. This might seem counter to our autonomous culture, but it will help bring a little sense to the SEO operations at TransferWise

Despite the possibility of a controller sometime down the road, autonomy is alive and well at TransferWise. I haven't seen or heard of this kind of culture in many organisations. It doesn't seem to be even a semi-common way of organisation. But for us, it has created both incredible business success and an incredible environment in which we work.

HOW A "SIMPLE" POINT OF VIEW MADE A £30,000/DAY DIFFERENCE

LUKE CARTHY

ECOMMERCE GROWTH CONSULTANT

Luke Carthy is a veteran of the digital marketing and eCommerce space. He worked in-house for seven years in roles such as Marketing and eCommerce Manager before becoming an independent consultant. He now helps digital clients harness SEO, conversion optimisation and strategy implementation to build sustainable, measurable eCommerce growth.

At first glance, this story has nothing to do with SEO.

But when you look deeper, it has everything to do with SEO. This incident several years ago encapsulated a mindset that I've tried to build ever since. And, it is something I believe every SEO expert should foster, especially when tackling problems that seem technical.

IS IT US... OR THEM?

I was working with an eCommerce company to improve their SEO. It was a small team, and we would occasionally hear about problems the other IT types were dealing with.

Our users were predominantly older folk aged 50 up, and often semi-retired. As a result, we took any issues and bugs they reported with a grain of salt. It was often a case of not knowing whether there was a genuine problem or if their lack of online savvy might be the cause.

Yet, there was one problem that kept getting reported three to four times every week. This happened over 12 to 18 months, and it persisted for a good reason: we couldn't replicate it. This worried us, because:

- If it was consistently reported by a few people, we could be sure a lot more were affected and not reporting.
- It was happening on the check-out page.

We knew we had a problem that could be costing the company a lot of revenue in failed orders, but we were not sure where to go from here.

A DIFFERENT POINT OF VIEW

The reported error message told people to call Sales, and a handful of times every week, people would do just that. One of our customer support team would raise a ticket, then pass to a developer. They'd investigate promptly, as checkout-related problems had high priority.

But this is as far as it would go. Developers would try to replicate with different card numbers, expiry dates and other values, but never see the bug. Nothing stood out in the logs. So it would stay unresolved... until the next report, where similar events would unfold.

I had listened to the calls and looked through various logs and data with no luck. Until one day, I took a different perspective to the problem.

We had configured our Google Analytics in a way that let us capture every error message on the site. So, I looked through those logs and discovered what appeared to be the error message customers were getting:

"Error 1007. Please call Sales on <Phone number>"

But what exactly did that mean for customers?

When I Googled "Error 1007" with the API we used, I found the answer. It simply meant the customer had entered an invalid credit card number, though you would never tell that by the message.

Knowing that, our developers updated the error to:

"Invalid card number. Please check your card number and try again".

Within 24 hours of making that 10-minute update, we saw an extra £30,000 in sales start to roll in on a daily basis. It now made sense: customers would see a message they understood, and then most likely check the number they had entered.

These incidents can be a huge win for both you and SEO at your company. By proving your focus on ROI (whether within the boundaries of SEO or beyond) lets you bank a lot of credits. This might translate into months or even years of unchallenged SEO recommendations, or extra access to developers to implement more of your ideas.

But beyond this important benefit, I took away three big lessons I am still conscious of today.

#1: TAKE THE CUSTOMER'S VIEWPOINT

The biggest takeaway I took from this episode was the "simplest".

Like developers, we SEO types often have to solve technical problems.

And like most developers, very few of us look at SEO from a customer focus.

The issue is that visitors to your site are not technical.

Of course, measures like traffic or keyword growth skew our perspective, but to the larger business, these things don't have much influence in isolation. CEOs and Managers want results in the form of revenue or profits. That means more than people finding a website, but customers pulling out their credit cards.

When you think of SEO beyond the data and in a "customer first" viewpoint, you naturally gravitate towards making life easier for them. 9 out of 10 times, a better experience for the customer affects the bottom line… and gives you the freedom to explore more of the things you want to.

#2: THE "SECRET" TO GETTING THINGS FIXED FAST

In the world of in-house SEO, you compete with other teams that all want precious time from the developers. But how do you get the time you need and get it prioritised?

Well, the not-so-secret secret is to prove the commercial value of a problem or task you have. It is easy to report a potential problem or log a request, but unless you can add context to the potential business impacts, your request ends up in a queue, like everything else. Whenever possible, I include the "commercial pain" with my reports, especially real dollar value or customer numbers affected. When it is painful enough, it encourages people to want it fixed right NOW.

Of course, you have to be able to set this up. The best way to do this: Google Analytics. Along with capturing error messages, our GA setup was also configured to capture the basket value for each session, regardless of whether it converted or was abandoned. And when putting your case forward, a report that shows an error message, number of people affected, and the lost basket value, is a potent weapon.

#3: MAKE THE MOST OF YOUR TOOLS

I just mentioned the power behind gathering extra data in Google Analytics to produce reports that highlight impacts. But while vanilla GA is good at giving insights and ideas to explore, you rarely get solid information you can act on. In this particular incident, out-of-the-box GA would not have caught the error messages — which proved the key to solving it — or lost basket values, as both needed extra configuration.

As an in-house SEO expert, this is exactly the sort of data I want: error messages, stock levels, price data and so on. When a problem rears its head or we need to deep dive into something, we have that visibility.

Capturing the data was relatively simple, taking no more than 15-20 minutes in GA and the data layer. It was another 10-minute task for the devs to add code that would pass any error message that fired to a custom variable in the data layer. Google Analytics shared the same variable, and would be able to access that data as a result.

CAPTURING LOST BASKET VALUE IN GOOGLE ANALYTICS

Setting up custom dimensions that let you trap customers' lost basket values (or any extra data) isn't difficult. Here's how:

Step 1: Create the custom definition you want to report on in GA. This is a simple task, and you can call it whatever you want, whether it's "lost basket value", "lost revenue" or a term that makes sense for your business. Make sure it's a session-based custom dimension.

Step 2: Create a new variable in GTM to handle the lost basket revenue data.

Step 3: Assign your new variable to your Google Analytics script in GTM. You can add this new variable to the custom dimensions section in your GA tag. Ensure that the variable index matches the custom dimension index in Google Analytics. This will ensure the data is passed to the right place when it reaches GA.

Step 4: Have your dev team pass the lost basket amount to your new variable via the data layer every time the basket total updates.

Step 5: Important — if a transaction is made, the lost basket value must be set to 0. As the basket was not lost. If a transaction did not take place during the session, then the lost basket value will remain as the last updated value.

You then have a way to capture potential lost revenue in Google Analytics!

BEYOND TACTICS: PRINCIPLES TO DRIVE STRATEGIC SEO

SIMON DANCE

SVP GROWTH, LYST.COM

Simon discovered SEO while working in the affiliate space. Having built a successful career in the field over the past 15 years, he is now a leader in the space. He has served as the Head of SEO (EU) for Amazon, Director of SEO for HouseTrip, and consulted for a number of high growth businesses, including Carwow and Domain. Simon is currently the SVP Growth for Lyst, an online platform that helps fashion lovers find exactly what they want.

For many in-house SEOs, tactics make up a big part of their approach.

There are hundreds of tactics, growth hacks and levers an SEO expert can pull, but these have become table stakes. I focused on evidence-based hypothesis design and alignment to customers, in order to unlock greater value for a business.

Of course, tactics have their place in SEO. However, if you want to make a real impact, you need more than a bag of tactical tricks.

THINK OF THE CUSTOMER

One of the biggest sins I see SEO teams commit is to focus on various levers they can pull. At best, they undervalue the customer. At worst, they completely disregard them. They obsess over SEO value, link juice and crawl budgets, and ignore almost everything else.

To put it bluntly, SEO tactics are the table stakes. Customers matter above all else. When you improve the customer experience, you grow the business. SEO might be the tool we use to achieve this, but our mission is no different from marketing, development, or brand teams.

I spent a big part of my first months at Lyst repositioning SEO towards customers and aligning with product teams already in that space. We became tight-knit with the user research and product design teams, and "customer first" became our mantra.

You get a very different reception when you say "we're doing this for customers" instead of "we're doing this for SEO". Teams and stakeholders are ready to get behind you, and the battle for resources becomes much easier.

GET THE LAY OF THE LAND

My first three months at Lyst were a busy time. I spent much of it understanding the problems we were looking to solve, rather than diving with assumption-driven plans or ideas.

For example, if we noticed customers were unhappy with a particular landing page template, we wanted to learn more. How could we improve that experience? By how much? What were hypotheses on specific actions we could take? What kind of impact would those actions have from a conversion rate, traffic or ranking perspective?

We would model these problems, sort them by potential impact from a business standpoint, and then think on how we could start on them.

It wasn't just the SEO challenges I looked at upon joining Lyst. I reviewed everything from team structure, individual team members, and roles. The review also included suppliers and anyone who might have a hand in our mission. I put everything on the table and critically assessed their role toward achieving our mission.

This meant tough decisions early on. If product features, team members and investments do not deliver value or hinder your ability to achieve our mission, then being decisive and standing by your decisions is required. For example, I ruthlessly cut projects which were distracting the team.

MAKING THE CASE FOR RESOURCES

When I arrived at Lyst, we had two dedicated SEO engineers. I knew that wasn't enough for our plans, so we built a case to get more.

We looked at existing traffic to identify problem spaces in the site where customers met an unsatisfactory experience. We then tied potential reasons, like poor conversion rate or bounce rate, to these problems. When we modelled projections off possible improvements, we could see the opportunities open to us.

We documented these problems in a Confluence page or Wiki, where we went into greater detail to come up with hypothesis-based tests. For example: "We believe these pages don't rank because of customer defects A, B or C. We believe there are 20 tasks we need to do. We will measure the success of each by running an A/B test".

These hypotheses were the catalyst to get in front of our leadership and present not just the opportunities, but an action plan that mapped out how we would use any investment.

We now have seven engineers working full-time on SEO projects.

It was a necessary cleaning of the decks to align the team with our new mission and make the trust and investment in SEO worthwhile.

INVEST IN THE RIGHT PEOPLE

Many in-house teams play the SEO game with only one or two people. That is nowhere near enough if you are playing to win big. A single person can take on two projects or experiments at most every month. Hard-working they might be, that kind of speed will never deliver the results bigger businesses need to compete. If you promise big results with increasing traffic and rankings, you need more support.

If a business is serious about SEO, they need to dedicate the resources. Naturally, every business is different, so what they can and should commit to SEO varies. But as a blanket statement, if a large business is unwilling to invest in at least two to three engineers, two SEO leaders, and one designer, there may be no point. That is not even counting Link Builders, Brand, Digital PR Resources or Content Creators, who may be better positioned in other teams.

BUILD YOUR IMPACT

When you secure more resources for SEO, the possibilities open up for you to embark on many more projects or activities. But there is an important qualifier that should preempt anything you want to do:

What value does this give to the customer?

Saying you need SEO content for a landing page is pointless if it offers little value.

Yet, I have seen several occasions where an SEO Lead wanted a dedicated content team, designers, and developers, all focused on SEO activities. This empire-building distracts from the customer-centric attitude that is the cornerstone of business success.

Regardless of the resources at your disposal, focus on building impact with other teams. Marketing teams want to reach and delight more customers. SEO remains a primary acquisition channel as customers have often been trained to start searches on a search engine.

In addition, working with other teams helps to create an unbeatable product or brand. Amazing SEO comes from a phenomenal product, high-quality marketing and outstanding customer experience. From my perspective, a strong brand will beat any SEO tactic in the long-term, no matter how clever the tactic is.

HAVE A SUCCESSION PLAN IN PLACE

Yes, I did just talk about growing your SEO team.

But my ultimate aspiration is for SEO to become less of a stand-alone role and more a part of product and technology teams. SEO should be woven into the DNA of a business and driven by technology and product teams. And while SEO specialists can be advocates for that, their presence can also work against integration.

If your SEO team is shrinking, you may not have to hit the panic button. SEO capability growing within core product and technology teams could more than offset this. For example, we are building a service which manages our XML sitemaps. Once done, that will be part of a technology stack our engineers maintain, rather than an SEO-specific task.

This comes back to building impact. Another way we do this is by sharing and spreading hypothesis-based test design with other teams, which speeds up how quickly we roll out SEO changes. Instead of a control-based structure where an SEO Manager approves everything, we now have a team of 30 odd SEOs, because the engineers and product teams all think about it.

I believe there will always be a role for SEO, no matter how pervasive it becomes in a business. That role might focus more on channel performance, with activities like monitoring the larger search ecosystem or watching competitor activity. If we can reduce routine tasks like site map management or basic audits, then these higher value activities will naturally come to the forefront.

***

The five principles I have discussed here are only the beginning. There is much more you can do to approach SEO from a principle-based perspective. But if you take one thing away, make it the first point: think Customer First. With this, any tactics or tricks you use have a context that elevates their effectiveness and your success with them.

HOW A BEST-PRACTICE GUIDEBOOK HAS HELPED THE TIMES AND THE SUNDAY TIMES TO SUCCEED WITH SEO

ALICE FOSTER
SEO EDITOR,
THE TIMES AND THE SUNDAY TIMES

Alice started out on a print newspaper in Cambodia and has spent more than a decade in journalism. Back in the UK, she worked across print and digital before evolving into an SEO journalist. Alice was previously SEO Content Editor at Express.co.uk and is currently SEO Editor at The Times and The Sunday Times. Based in two fast-paced newsrooms, she leads the SEO team and works to get great quality journalism to the top of Google.

How do you bring two of the world's oldest newspapers into the digital age? From my experience, you need a change in digital culture and technical innovation to go hand in hand.

Five years ago, there was no SEO editor for our website and no efforts were made to optimise stories for Google. This was because we worked with a paywall that kicked in for readers and crawlers after the first hundred words, so we struggled to rank highly because Googlebot could not get through our gates.

Back then, Google's controversial First Click Free policy forced subscription websites to offer a number of articles for free each day in exchange for having their pages crawled in full. We had taken a stand, refused to take part and virtually disappeared from search results as a result.

That all changed when Google ended First Click Free in October 2017.

News Corp chief executive Robert Thomson said its demise was "an important first step in recognising the value of legitimate journalism and provenance on the Internet".

We implemented Google's replacement policy, Flexible Sampling, which let us decide how much, if any, content we put outside the paywall. But it was not enough for Google to change its rules, the change had to be accompanied by a shift in culture in the newsrooms.

My predecessor Taneth Evans introduced new search approaches, rolled out training and integrated SEO into editorial processes in 2017. I joined Taneth's team as one of two SEO journalists in January 2018 and took over as editor in November that year, after she was promoted to head of audience development.

Our website hit a new record for search traffic in November 2019, and this would not have been possible without a change of mindset towards SEO across the newsrooms. It was just as important as the end of First Click Free.

I found that writing an SEO guide for the editorial floors was an effective way to bring on board and engage our journalists. I made sure that it didn't contain jargon and explained our best practice in clear, straightforward language.

All newsrooms have style guides and the ones at The Times and The Sunday Times are particularly revered. You can even buy The Times Style Guide, which is described as "an indispensable guide to the use of correct English".

Journalists refer to style guides in the course of their work, and I wanted to set down our SEO best practice in a similar format. While writing the guide, I worked alongside editors and sub-editors to come up with our own unique approach to SEO.

Through the consultation process, I built relationships across the newsrooms and continued the conversation about how SEO should be integrated. I then rolled out the guide by organising training sessions based on its principles.

Of course, editorial SEO cannot work without technical SEO. If you have the best editorial practices in the world, technical issues can stop you from ranking highly. Conversely, you might have a perfect website but you still need to create the right content.

Allowing Googlebot through our paywall helped the search engine understand our journalism better. Creating an SEO guide helped our journalists to understand Google and the way it works better too.

HOW TO WIN FRIENDS AND INFLUENCE PEOPLE: SEO EDITION

DAVID GERRARD
TEAM LEAD SEO, HEYCAR

David fell into digital marketing after completing university. After a year of working in paid search, he discovered SEO and never looked back. He spent six years in three different agencies, leading SEO for a wide portfolio of clients. Wanting a change, he jumped ship to become the in-house Team Lead SEO for heycar, an online auto marketplace based in Berlin.

Like many in-house SEOs, I'm an agency "defector". I spent around six years handling SEO for agency clients before landing at heycar, a German-based marketplace for buying and selling used cars.

As you may know, there are big differences between agency and in-house, the biggest being the depth I can get into working in-house. With agencies, I had a portfolio of clients to jump between, which made complex, time-consuming work difficult. At heycar, I can get my head into deep technical projects because I have the time.

There is one big similarity between working on both sides: **Relationships are key.** However, when you are agency-side, you often work with client contacts who do much of the relational heavy lifting for you. As an in-house SEO, it is up to you to form the bonds and get the buy-in for the help and support you need.

CONVERTING THE MASSES

People being skeptical about SEO is not a new problem. There is also a perception that SEO is tucked away in a corner, and pops up only to interrupt other teams.

More importantly, other teams might think your tampering will derail or ruin their projects. While rarely the case, it is a view you may have to debunk. The best way to do this not just prove SEO's value (and your own) to the business, but to form strong alliances and build real relationships.

These were six of the methods I applied at heycar.

Focus on the business reason

Everybody in the business knows the key business targets and metrics we have. For example, one of our core objectives is to continuously lower cost per lead and this can be unsustainable when supported solely by paid channels.

When I joined heycar, I framed SEO to show what it could achieve long-term, highlighting the potential to drive down costs and help hit several strategic business goals. Presenting SEO this way had an educational advantage: it dispelled ideas that SEO was only keyword research or other activities that were seen as lower-value. When I presented an accurate picture of the benefits behind SEO, it corrected false impressions that it was a single discipline with limited value.

Build a roadmap everyone can see

Planning is one of the first things you do at a new company. But as vital as a well-made SEO strategy is, sharing that plan is perhaps even more so.

Soon after I joined, I sat down with the product managers to walk them through my SEO roadmap. It wasn't a complicated process; we reviewed the list, pointed out cross-overs in terms of mutual interest, and I asked for their input. It was a simple exercise, but it paid off as both teams lined up projects where they could support each other.

At heycar, we have a dynamic roadmap for all teams. Anyone can see what SEO has planned, and I can see what marketing or the developers have in store. This gives me another opportunity to help others and show value. I look through team plans, find projects relevant to SEO, and then work out how I can help get those initiatives over the line.

Set OKRs that share success

Like many companies, we use the OKR framework to define objectives. Pioneered by Intel and made popular by Google, this performance measurement framework measures whether an individual or a team has achieved previously stated, quantifiable results.

While SEO has its own OKRs, I saw these as a chance to partner more closely with other teams.

Aligning OKRs was a natural process with some teams, like product management. One of their objectives is improving conversion rate, and they conduct a lot of CRO and testing on features to do this. This opened the door for SEO. I approached them on how to make their tests more accurate by driving higher volumes to the pages they wanted. We could also shape the intent of that traffic to maximise the number of qualified visits.

I helped set them up for success... just as they helped the SEO team hit our OKRs.

Another instance was an objective we set with one of the development teams to achieve 10% of the visibility our biggest competitor enjoys. heycar competes against more-established players, and incremental steps like this are important. SEO would be hard pressed to accomplish by itself, but sharing this goal meant we didn't have to.

Communicate updates, results, and praise

Processes, plans and goals weren't the only things I shared with other teams.

Every project has a different timeline, from a couple of days to months. That doesn't mean we get support from other teams, thank them, and disappear into the night. We keep them in the loop with updates, so they know their assistance didn't just evaporate.

Sharing progress reports has helped build rapport, but this was reinforced by sharing successes. When we confirm results, I happily send out an all hands email to highlight the role people played in the achievement. It is a small thing that shows we value their support, which makes the marketing team, product managers or developers more ready to help when I approach them with another project.

Spread the word on SEO

Before people can jump onboard SEO, they have to understand what it really is and what it can do for them. So educating others was another of the first things I did at heycar.

Fortunately, there were two forums set up to let me do that. The first was a Lunch and Learn event, where I presented SEO to others in a casual environment. I believe this was one of the most beneficial things I did early on. Yes, it helped educate others and banish some false impressions around SEO, but it also introduced me to many of the people I would work with.

The second avenue was a request to the CEO to present to the board. I wasn't trying to be pushy, but wanted to be up-front with the potential of SEO, how long it could take, and what I had planned. Again, this was an opportunity to put a face on SEO with the senior stakeholders in the company. heycar had regular meetings where team members could do this, so I took the advantage to start getting senior buy-in.

Grab a coffee and chat

You might have noticed a common thread in what I have discussed: communication.

Emphasise team cooperation, find mutual interest in common goals, get others to weigh in your roadmap, share results and praise generously... it all comes down to communicating with others.

That is why I am always ready to talk with people. That might mean to grab a coffee for half an hour, or a 2-minute chat at their desk. Either way,

I try to talk face-to-face as much as possible and not rely on digital tools like Slack. I want to be present and focused on the other person, because so many today don't do that.

LIKE SEO, RESULTS DON'T COME INSTANTLY

I'm happy I defected to in-house SEO. Being able to dedicate more time to projects, dig deeper into the industry I am part of, and add longer-term value instead of quick wins are all big advantages of being in-house.

But I needed allies if heycar's SEO was going to succeed, and forming alliances and strengthening bonds with other stakeholders wouldn't happen instantly. So, I concentrated on what I could do to build relationships.

1. Focusing on the business reason
2. Building a roadmap everyone can see
3. Setting OKRs that share success
4. Communicating updates, results, and praise
5. Spreading the word on SEO
6. Grabbing a coffee and chatting

It has been almost two years since I landed in Berlin to join heycar. We have had some good wins, but there is still plenty of work to do. The main difference today is that I have the relationships and the backing I need to see an even more ambitious round of SEO initiatives through.

NECESSARY EVIL TO NOTABLE EDGE: OPTIMISING FILTER PAGES FOR RANKING AND CONVERSION

ALINA GHOST
SEO MANAGER, AMARA

Alina discovered SEO when she began copywriting. After two years at Carpetright, she moved deeper into digital marketing, working for Debenhams before stepping into a more consultancy-based role as Marketing Manager at Tesco. She moved on to become SEO Manager for Amara where she led a team of five. Alina currently runs a podcast called "SEO With Mrs Ghost", where she discusses industry topics with other leading SEO figures.

Filter pages are part of life for most e-commerce sites.

Many sites block hundreds of thousands, if not millions, of these pages from indexing because they add no value. The only thing 99% of them are good for is blowing out crawl budget and creating duplicate content issues if done incorrectly.

However, not all filter pages are useless. In fact, a project we ran through 2019 proved how valuable these pages could be to an e-commerce site.

FILTER PAGES 101

Filter pages are variations of product listing pages, and occur when a user applies one or more filters to a product category. At Amara — the online only interiors site I manage SEO for — we use filters like these:

- Product Type
- Colour
- Material
- Style
- Design

For products that come in different colours, sizes and styles, the number of combinations can spiral out. When you account for the range of products any larger e-commerce site has, the sheer volume of filter pages presents a huge problem.

Most sites typically solve this by blocking filter pages from indexation using their robots.txt file, as we did. But we eventually realised these pages gave us an opportunity.

A SIMPLE PROCESS

It started with research.

We investigated long tail keywords relevant to Amara products and their search volumes, and then chose those with the most potential. After removing the code on robots.txt that disallowed filter pages to be crawled or indexed, we added 'noindex, nofollow' to each page's head. This allowed us to choose which filters to make visible to Google to attract relevant and valuable traffic.

That wasn't to say we indexed every filter page for a particular product, which could number in the thousands. It was a set of pages we thought would bring relevant traffic if we indexed them. Making the changes were simple, albeit time consuming: our custom-built website platform allowed us to set the page's index status with a couple of clicks.

This careful indexing continued over seven months. We followed the same process: find keywords we wanted to target, unblock relevant pages for indexing, and monitor their performance. Once those pages appeared in the rankings, we saw them make a phenomenal difference to our visibility and conversion.

COPY THAT CATAPULTED RANKINGS

At first, we indexed pages as they were. Our site systems allowed for automated titles and URLs that alphabetised no matter the journey taken to find the filtered product type. We didn't have time to add anything extra to the pages at first, but after a month or two, we made an important change.

We found that even though our indexed filter pages would reach the first page of rankings, they lingered at the bottom. We wanted them to rank in the top three spots to gain the extra clicks . So, we systematically added a high-quality sentence or two about the product, including a reference to the long-tail term we were targeting.

The copy sent our pages soaring up the search rankings. Many filter pages hit the top three within a few days of adding this brief copy. It sometimes also had the welcome bonus of expanding the number of keywords associated with the page.

THE PAGES PAY OFF

When we wrapped up the project, the numbers showed we had:

- Indexed over 2,000 filter pages on the site
- Added copy to over 650 of those pages
- Achieved rankings for almost 1,300 keywords

The results have been impressive. While many of the pages rank for long-tail, low traffic terms, their particular niche often sees high conversion rates. One page enjoyed a conversion rate of around 10%!

More importantly, the filter pages have made a substantial difference to Amara's bottom line, increasing organic revenue by 400% period-vs-period (the 7 months of the project), and 250% year-on-year. For an SEO project that was relatively simple in terms of technical sophistication, it more than delivered a first-rate investment on our effort.

Considering most see these pages as not adding value to SEO, being able to convert them into revenue generators was a big win for Amara.

Note: I would like to thank my former SEO Assistant at Amara, Ellen Blacow (@ellenblacow) for putting a lot of time and effort into this project.

REDUCING RISK WITH AUTOMATED SEO TESTING

BEN JOHNSON
FREELANCE SEO CONSULTANT

Ben got his first taste of SEO with Sky's graduate programme. From then on, he immersed himself in the world of SEO, whether it was growing one of the largest history sites in the UK or managing SEO for an online start-up. These days, Ben is a freelance SEO consultant and co-founder of SiteKite.io, an automated SEO testing tool.

Every time a deployment came around, I struggled to sleep that night.

The company I worked for - a property portal website - deployed updates to their site every two weeks. Each time, there was always the risk of something SEO-related breaking unexpectedly. One release might accidentally drop the index tags, while another might mess up the canonical logic.

The potential impacts of SEO going awry were huge for this FTSE 250 company. As the Head of SEO, any fallout ended up on my head, but the risk of missing something with manual crawls and inspections — no matter how many we did — was apparent. I had to find a better way to check the site's technical SEO before a release.

A BETTER WAY OF SEO TESTING, VERSION 1

Anyone who has been in SEO for even a couple of months is familiar with Screaming Frog or Sitebulb crawls. In fact, we often spend a lot of our time crawling environments to make sure the existing SEO and any changes survive a release intact.

Personally, I have three problems with the "typical" approach:

1. Manually reviewing crawls is error-prone, and minor changes can often fly under the radar.
2. We spend far too long conducting crawls when we could be doing other, more valuable tasks.
3. Manual crawls are a reactive way of testing SEO and puts us on the back foot immediately.

Searching for a better way to handle SEO testing led me to what I labelled my "Version 1" solution.

It was a Chrome extension for our developers and software testers to install in their browser. Built for our staging and QA environments, I programmed it with a number of SEO rules. It would run in the background as devs or testers navigated our site. If the extension found an SEO error on a page, it showed a warning at the bottom right of the browser and prompted the user to contact me.

The rules themselves were rudimentary. They were worded like "on these types of pages, I expect there to be canonicals that point to themselves", "I don't expect any no-index tags on this page" and so on.

While the extension wasn't perfect, it was a huge step forward. It allowed me to "recruit" others to help with SEO testing, reduce the reliance on manual crawls, and even find bugs we weren't specifically looking for.

A BETTER WAY OF SEO TESTING, VERSION 2

As much as "Version 1" was a leap in improving our SEO testing, there were a few shortfalls:

- You couldn't force devs or testers to install the extension, short of standing at their desk and asking directly.
- When devs or testers navigated the sites, they wouldn't always visit the most important URLs for SEO, especially on larger sites.
- Some parts of the site built solely for SEO would rarely be looked at by anyone else, such as robots.txt, sitemap.xml or redirects in .htaccess.

When I moved to my next company, I wanted to improve on the idea and tackle these problems. However, there was a second reason behind this upgrade. My new employers ran on a continuous deployment cycle, which meant more releases, more often. Manual crawls would never be enough to keep up with the rate of releases, and so posed a high risk.

So, I developed "Version 2": a fully automated SEO test suite. Based on JavaScript technology, it was a series of tests scheduled to run every 12 hours and report the results.

The tests themselves were in a format similar to Version 1:

- "I expect the home page does not include no-index tags."
- "I expect our location landing pages to talk about the location they're targeting."

A TECH STACK FOR AUTOMATED SEO TESTING

While I have seen very few others build their own SEO test suites, there is no reason you cannot do the same. Some of the technology is a little out-dated now, but let me run you through the technology stack I used for "Version 2".

Node.js

This is an open-source, cross-platform runtime environment, and is what the test code ran off.

PhantomJS

For your tests to run, they need to hit your site. To do that, you need a browser. PhantomJS is a "headless" browser: it has no visible GUI. This makes it faster to execute, so you can get through more tests faster.

(Note: Development stopped on PhantomJS in 2018. There are other browsers you can use to run your tests, such as Chrome, which offers a headless version.)

CasperJS

Finally, you need a way to write your tests. I used CasperJS, a browser navigation and testing framework built to run with PhantomJS.

(Note: Yet again, CasperJS is no longer actively maintained. However, you can use another option like Selenium, one of the most common and well-documented testing frameworks available.)

If you are already familiar with JavaScript, a basic test suite could be up and running with around 20-30 hours of work. Obviously, if you have to learn JS, it will take somewhat longer!

The suite was populated with literally thousands of these rules. If a test found a problem, it would report by sending an email and a Slack notification. Again, the reporting conveyed the essential details for us to follow up: the web page it ran on, the expected result, and the actual result.

BEYOND THE BASICS

Version 2 was a godsend. The code base was going through constant updates, refactoring and changes to the database. Sometimes we would find pages completely removed that we wouldn't have known without the automated testing. Other times, the canonical logs failed, while on one occasion a site-wide no-index tag was almost deployed, which would have been a disaster.

However, running these kinds of tests help you to pick more than just SEO problems. A lot of the time, you can detect UI issues. For example, when migrating from PHP to a more AJAX-style front-end, we kept running into rendering problems. The SEO tests picked these up immediately, as pages loaded but no content displayed.

The other advantage to an automated suite is that once you have the essentials covered, you can add more tests to cover more parts of the site. Here are a couple of suggestions you can build into your suite:

- Check that images load.
- Check server response time for page loads.
- Check TTFB speeds.

Implement a robust test suite, and you will see the results for yourself. If for no other reason, having your SEO automatically inspected every day or so will help you sleep at night... it did for me!

READY-MADE TOOLS TO TUNE UP YOUR TESTING

Because of its success at saving our SEO, and because I had seen automated testing used so rarely, I decided to make Version 2 publicly available. The end result was SiteKite.io: a subscription-based SaaS tool that minimises coding and configuration so you can create tests almost immediately.

Of course, nothing stops you developing your own framework, and in some situations that may be the best way to do, since you have complete control over it. However, if you want the testing but don't have the resources or availability to code it up, an external tool like SiteKite may be perfect for you.

There are other options available that can help you keep tabs on your SEO without having to spend the time and effort conducting manual crawls.

Little Warden

This is great for monitoring different aspects of your website, like sitemaps, content, and indexability. It goes beyond SEO, as it also checks for things domain and SSL certificate expiration, as well as malware.

Content King

Content King is another option worth looking at. As the name implies, you're able to keep an eye on your content and make sure changes to it are not affecting your SEO.

DATA-LED JOURNALISM: HOW WE CREATED PAGES MORE PEOPLE WANTED TO READ

JONATHAN JONES
FORMER ORGANIC PERFORMANCE LEAD, MONEYSUPERMARKET GROUP

Jonathan started his first business — a free web hosting service — at the age of 16. To build his client base, he learned SEO and never looked back. After joining an agency where he worked with several big brands like Toyota and Natwest, Jonathan jumped to in-house SEO with MoneySuperMarket. He has recently taken a position as the Director of SEO with Forbes.

Back in 2010, Sir Tim Berners-Lee, inventor of the World Wide Web, spoke about journalism in the modern era.

His point was simple. With data everywhere, journalists and writers couldn't ignore it any longer. They had to be comfortable using data to find stories. In simple terms, they had to become "data journalists". And as we looked to update hundreds of pages of out-dated content, we realised we had to do the same as today's journalists.

LOOKING PAST THE LANDING PAGES

MoneySuperMarket's site revolves around several key landing pages on topics like car insurance, mortgages, and life insurance. The main landing pages alone drive over half of our organic traffic in their respective areas. They're well-designed, have the kind of content visitors who are in the mindset to purchase and get regular updates from the content team. For the hundreds of thousands that land on our site each month, the pages are a perfect introduction to MoneySuperMarket.

We also have hundreds of guide pages. These are more informational, such as focusing on the best mortgage to apply for and similar topics. When I first started, these pages hadn't been touched for years and had been neglected. Many had not been updated since 2011, and the timestamps on each page said as much.

The reason behind this neglect was a company attitude that focused on looking forward. The vast majority of our efforts were on building new content or updating higher volume pages. Even though the guide pages delivered a hefty amount of traffic, they weren't considered important enough to warrant updating as other pages were converting at a higher rate and therefore there was no reason to focus on those guides. However we believed that this was having an impact on MoneySuperMarket's overall perception as often the guidance on these pages were outdated.

That was something I wanted to change.

DATA-LED JOURNALISM

For MoneySuperMarket, content has always been a staple. In late 2017, I wanted to find out how we could create more engaging, attention-grabbing content at scale.

Typically, we didn't do much in-depth research for our pages. Content writers were told "here is the product, here are the features", then left to their own devices. They might do some basic research when writing the article, but that would be it. We wanted to take that to a more sophisticated level.

We started what we called "data-led journalism". It is not a novel technique in any sense, but it was a new approach for us. Our data science team was a key part of this, as they could pull data around what people did on the site, what types of products they bought, reasons for buying, and other details. Once we got the data, we would investigate patterns or questions behind common searches, find a great story, and then bring it to life on the page.

A "BLACK BOX" PROOF OF CONCEPT

To prove data-led journalism could create engaging content that drove SEO, we tested the concept on a smaller page. This was our telematics, or black box car insurance page.

Telematics is when an insurer installs a device in your car to monitor driving habits, which affect how much you pay in premiums. We started with this page as it was a little different and we had a lot of data we could use. For example, we pointed out that customers could save £300 if they took out a black box insurance policy over a standard one.

The proof of concept worked, and we saw traffic rise off the back of our data-driven changes. As a bonus, we received some great coverage in the national press. With this page a success, it was time to scale.

AN AGILE APPROACH TO SCALING

Proving that data-led journalism could work on a single page was one thing. Rolling out that approach across 500 pages that made up a big part of our traffic generation was another.

The first challenge was to convince other business teams, who were worried by the scale of our project. Luckily, we could back up our proposals with data. The numbers showed the revenue opportunities available if we followed through, which helped secure buy-in from senior stakeholders.

Finding a process to encourage collaboration between all the teams was another significant obstacle. We convinced the data science team to regularly give us data, which we would then analyse to find popular questions and hot topics. The next step was to write content around the best findings. With only three content writers on staff, we had to outsource to freelancers to help scale.

When we started, the process was very lightweight. For example:

1. We would create a brief for the content team, on which the article was to be based.
2. The writer might need to go to the data science team for more data.

AGILE VS WATERFALL

If you have worked with software development teams, you are probably familiar with the Agile and Waterfall methodologies. For this project, we used Agile, which is a stark contrast to the more rigid Waterfall traditionally used.

Waterfall

Waterfall is a linear approach to completing projects. The project flows through a series of distinct steps, like data gathering, analysis, content creation, page design, and so on. Planning with Waterfall locks in every step from start to finish, and one step has to finish before the next one begins. If something big comes in while completing a Waterfall project, you often have to say "no" because you have your plan.

Agile

Agile is a lighter-weight, iterative approach to development. Planning still occurs, but Agile allows you to respond to changing requirements or circumstances as they happen. For this project, we wanted to stay nimble and adapt if opportunities popped up or new priorities appeared.

3. Once they had written the article, the writer sent it to the design team to build a mock.
4. The compliance team would check the page (though these become more periodic audits).
5. The publishing team would then build the page and release it.

This covered the larger inter-team process, but there were still individual processes that we had to adapt to. This wasn't necessarily a problem, as we adopted an Agile approach for the project.

STAYING ONE STEP AHEAD

When I joined MoneySuperMarket, we were creating very standard pages and putting the emphasis on link building. With this project, we flipped the script: we created high-quality content that was engaging and useful for customers. Thanks to the better content, we not only increased engagement, but also the number of links to our site without any extra effort on our part.

The project ran from late 2017 through to early 2018. From around March, we started to see the fruits of our labour. Google rewarded us with the top ranking for key head terms: life insurance, car insurance, travel insurance, credit cards, mortgages, and loans. This was the best result for SEO we had ever seen in the history of MoneySuperMarket.

In early 2019, we received the ultimate compliment: our competitors copied our data-led journalism for their own content. So, while they are playing "catch up", we are already busy thinking of what's next.

THE PENGUIN PROGNOSTICATOR: GOING AGAINST THE CROWD

ANTONIS KONSTANTINIDIS

HEAD OF SEO, EF ENGLISH LIVE

Helping Betfair's Greek blog attract more traffic was Antonis' introduction to the world of SEO. Since then, he has worked primarily in SEO leadership roles throughout Europe and the UK. Antonis currently works for EF English Live as their Head of SEO and Content Marketing.

Sooner or later, it catches up to you. In this case, "it" was Google.

If you were part of the SEO world before 2012, you might remember the frenzy of spammy link-building and link manipulation that went on then. Websites could influence rankings with "black hat" techniques, push low-quality websites far higher than where they would normally rank. It was a huge problem, but one I predicted wouldn't last for long.

PRIOR TO PENGUIN

In one of my previous positions, it was our goal to rank #1 for a number of keywords in the industry. Yet in the pre-Penguin world, links and rankings worked somewhat differently to today.

Links and anchor text had a higher value during this era of the Internet and were reasonably easy to tamper with: two attributes that made SEO vulnerable to exploitation. With some willing partner websites and carefully tailored anchor text, it wasn't hard to have your site — regardless of quality — rank on the first page, if not at #1.

But nothing on the World Wide Web stands still for long. Google's war on low-quality and spammy links erupted with the Penguin updates.

GOING AGAINST THE CROWD

My strategy was the opposite to what most of the industry did prior to the Google algorithm updates. We ignored manipulating anchor text or grabbing as many links that we could, and instead focused on building our brand.

Naturally, links were (and still are) an important part of SEO, so we still wanted to do link-building. But we did this through natural relationships, rather than play with link text or other manipulative techniques. It was more a PR-style strategy: we promoted content and pushed it out to other high-quality sites, but we let those sites decide for themselves what links and anchor text they used.

Another big part of our strategy was a willingness to wait. We had confidence in our brand, and perhaps felt we deserved to hold the top ranking for several keywords. The reality of the time said otherwise, but this didn't faze us. In the meantime, we worked on other improvements to strengthen our SEO over the mid to long-term.

SELLING A COUNTER-INTUITIVE APPROACH

There are two big risks when you go against what is accepted, and it was no different in the SEO world back in 2012.

1. People question you, and perhaps even think you are stupid.

2. If you are wrong, a lot of pressure lands on your shoulders.

I was sure the tide would turn, but I had to sell my wait-it-out strategy to others in the business who thought "get 100 links with the #1 keyword as the anchor text, and the #1 ranking is ours". It sounds like a tempting proposition, and it was difficult to argue against. But my position didn't waver: yes, we could take top spot… but end up on page two six months later.

You know too well that people want to tap into the power of SEO, but don't understand many of the ideas and actions behind it. In a way, us in-house SEOs are like an agency, in that we need to sell ourselves and what we do regularly.

There were two major things I did to help sell this "against the crowd" approach.

Advise on the risks

It is important to advise about the dangers of going down a particular road. No business wants to deal with the threat of a Google penalty, so you have to spell out what one could mean to your company.

Note: If people don't believe a Google penalty could happen to them, point out how Google penalised Chrome — their own web browser — over a 2014 sponsored post campaign. The penalty knocked Chrome off the first page for searches like "browser".

This is part of your role as an SEO, though it is rarely brought up. You are the driving force for all things SEO, but at times you also have to be the brake.

Show small improvements

Just because I didn't play the game everyone else played in 2012 didn't mean I sat on my hands. There were other things I did to help grow rankings

VOICE SEARCH: ANOTHER EXAMPLE OF THE "CROWD"

In SEO, staying well-informed comes with the job. Whether you read blogs, follow key players on social media or watch YouTube videos is less important than who you get your information from. Choose the right people and you get plenty of clues of what is coming. If I had to recommend one person, Bill Slawski would be at the top of the list.

Take the hot topic of voice search, for instance. So many weigh in on it and make recommendations to survive the "age of voice search". These reports gained momentum, and now blogs everywhere talk about how different voice search is. Yet, a couple of people inside Google (including names like Gary Illyes) have stated on Twitter there is little you can do to optimise for voice search. So long as Google understands the voice query, the search algorithm works in a similar way to a typed query. Voice searches — excepting queries from devices like Google Home — even get logged in Search Console like any other query.

This is something you are responsible for as an SEO Manager: doing your own research, interpreting the situation and reading between the lines. At the very least, conduct your due diligence rather than just following the latest fad.

and traffic, as well as position our site to capitalise on the anticipated post-Penguin world of rankings.

In my experience, "big" keywords change positions slowly. It is typically easier to jump up the SERPs with long-tail keywords. This is what I focused on during that period: building my employer's brand against many long-tail keywords, which netted us small improvements I showed others while we prepared for bigger moves over the next year or so.

"CRYSTAL BALLING" THE FUTURE

This episode might be old, but the approach towards SEO remains relevant today. As an SEO, you shouldn't always follow the latest trend or loudest voices, because they may well be wrong. Google has run experiments, drawn up plans, and made decisions years ago on how the algorithm will work in coming years.

Instead, act like a genuine SEO leader. Do these and you will less likely be fooled and more likely to stay ahead of the pack:

1. Follow a handful of the right people in the industry, and ignore what everyone else says.

2. Keep up-to-date and look for clues for which way the field might turn next.
3. Make your own plans and decisions on how to handle SEO.
4. Nail down the SEO fundamentals and make small improvements if the time is not right to launch a major initiative.

While you may not have a crystal ball, you will be able to foresee the future of SEO in some small way. When you can do that, you can take advantage of things other SEOs never see coming, and become an SEO "fortune teller" for your business.

THINK LAND GRAB: CAREER ADVICE FOR SEOS AND THEIR EMPLOYERS

NEIL MIDDLEMASS
FOUNDER AND CAREER PARTNER, ASSEMBL

Neil has been hiring into the digital market for 15 years, with a specialisation of helping businesses to build, scale or in-house their performance marketing teams. Neil is the co-founder of Assembl, a disruptive hiring solution that aims to fix a broken recruitment market model. The platform uses intelligent automation technology, a dynamic fee structure, and in-person expertise to deliver a hiring solution tailored to the complexities of the modern market.

If you're looking at in-housing SEO, you need to attract good people. The question is: will good people want the job you're creating?

It is not all down to money: expectations change as people progress in their careers, so what works for junior hires won't necessarily work for more senior hires, and vice versa.

If you are an SEO specialist considering an in-house position, it is worth evaluating the role objectively before you move forward.

EVALUATING IN-HOUSE JOBS

Generally speaking, the most successful SEO careers begin agency-side. Our data shows that agencies are better at mobilising talent, so career progression is generally faster agency-side. On top of this, agencies offer exposure to multiple clients with differing business challenges and objectives.

In the last 12 months, around a third of all agency-side SEO specialists leaving their company have moved in-house. As in-housing becomes more viable and more prevalent, there are many more in-house options for the SEO specialist.

Of course, not all in-house jobs are created equal.

With that the case, how do you tell which roles are more likely to give you the success and satisfaction you want?

Digital first

One of the first things to look for is how intrinsic SEO is to the business. Is it a core function of their operations, or more of an after-thought? As a generalisation, you find better SEO jobs at digital-centric businesses, simply for the reason they are more reliant on it. As a result, you get better executive sponsorship, which means more resources and buy-in.

Your boss-to-be

The next thing to consider: your boss. Who are you reporting to? What do they know about SEO? What do they think they know about SEO? A Head of Digital whose idea of SEO is just links and content could constrain how successful you are in the role. Ideally, you want remit to push SEO at a senior level through the business, or to work for someone who has your back if you are not moving into a senior position.

PREPARE AN EXIT PLAN

SEO is not a job for life. This might seem like an unusual thing to say in a book about SEO, but the most successful moves capitalise on lateral mobility within businesses.

SEO is still treated as a specialist 'channel' by many businesses, and this can restrict the influence and impact of the role of the SEO. Career paths in SEO are less linear than paths from other digital marketing specialisms, and there are generally fewer opportunities to broaden exposure as opposed to paid media counterparts.

How is SEO defined within the business and what are the opportunities to broaden your remit? This is something else I encourage people moving in-house to consider before deciding. **Look for the land grab.**

So, go beyond your original role. This might mean content, UX, marketing or paid media. If you have a technical bent, you might work on technical projects outside of SEO. If you are product-focused, you could look to product development, while content specialists might take on brand work. Building and cashing in personal brand equity will also help here, so make sure you join a business where you are prepared to invest and put down roots.

Employers have to think about this too if they want to attract high performers.

ACCOMMODATE EXIT PLANS

If you need an SEO, set them up for both business and personal success. Give them opportunities to make a land grab. Most talented people are not satisfied with a fancier title and a little more cash if their role doesn't give them a path to genuinely develop.

This has to be flexible, because it depends on the person. Fortunately, SEO has a strong visibility across much of the business. A typical in-house SEO has to know the products so they can find the best keywords and queries for the site. They have to talk to tech teams. They need to know what content drives more traffic, and often know the website better than anyone else in the business. Most SEOs have a wide range of skills, so you have to think what you can do with someone like that.

Assembl's Foresite report backs this up: in-house SEOs will move. There is great appetite in the market to shift into different roles that enhance someone's skills beyond SEO. If you can offer that, you are in a prime position to attract first-class talent.

HANDLE MARKET INFLATION & EXPERIENCE GAPS

The SEO job market has grown a lot over the last 15 years. Much of that is agency-led, in that more SEOs work in agencies than in-house (at least in the London market). Nevertheless, the high demand for people and comparatively low supply has created inflationary conditions in the market.

Despite inflationary conditions, the data shows agency salaries in the SEO market haven't changed much over the last 10 years. As a result, agencies are leaking SEO talent:

- 35% go in-house.
- 10% start freelancing.
- 5% move overseas.
- 4% switch into cross-channel roles.
- 3% leave the market completely.

This has affected the size of the available talent pool and has meant that agencies have had to either promote more quickly or hire external talent to step up into a more senior role. Our data suggests that nearly 75% of all SEO specialists moving between agencies do so into a more senior position.

Salary levels may not have changed, but progression rate has increased and the market has become more junior. In other words, instead of inflating, the market has done the opposite: it has *compressed*.

This situation has killed the market at Senior Executive level. They are very hard for in-house teams to recruit, because the progression is so good on the agency side.

The most successful recruitment strategies include a management layer with experience training and leading teams, with entry-level roles beneath this. This way, businesses can shop for skills and not rely on shortfalls in the market. This helps to deal with both inflation and availability gaps in the market. Plus, you develop a much stronger SEO team built exactly around what you need.

FINAL ADVICE

For SEOs: Building your career plan isn't gloom and doom. Few people spend their entire career in one field, and this goes double for the Digital disciplines. The only difference with SEO is that you may need to plan your exit plan more carefully. Ensure you can land grab and broaden your skill set to take advantage of any big career opportunities sometime down the road.

For businesses: Attracting talent is a two-way street. If you want the best knocking on your door, you have to create the right conditions. Needless to say, ongoing training and development are crucial components of retention, especially in a fast-moving and knowledge-intensive area such as SEO. And if you find the right person or build a winning team, you will reap the benefits.

(Note from Simon Schnieders: The Blue Array Academy has been designed to offer the training, development and certification in-house or agency staff need to really take their careers to the next level. For businesses it's also a great retention tool as well as being ROI focused with actionable techniques beginning on day one. Find out more at www.bluearrayacademy.com).

THE OVERKILL APPROACH TO SCORING YOUR DREAM SEO ROLE

ORIT MUTZNIK

HEAD OF SEO, SILKFRED

Orit jumped into SEO over 11 years ago, and has been leading SEO teams since 2011. After leading eToro's SEO department for two years, she moved from Tel Aviv to London in 2018 to head up SilkFred's SEO efforts. Her other skills include ASO, Content Marketing and Digital Marketing.

I have a confession to make: I love London.

I fell in love after one visit to this great city. And I decided I wanted to live there.

Being in Israel made the move a little more challenging. If I was going to move to London, I would have to find a company willing to look at me, even though I was thousands of kilometres away.

BURST THROUGH THE DOOR

With more than a decade in SEO and my then-current role as Head of SEO for a major online trading company, my prospects were promising. But with my geographical limitation, I knew I had to do more than most candidates if I was to win a job offer.

If a company opened the door even a little for me, I would have to burst in. That is how I do things professionally, and it is what won me other positions, so there was no reason to change that attitude.

When I found an opening for Head of SEO at SilkFred, I went for it.

FIRST HURDLE: THE AUDIT

As part of the application process, candidates had to provide a list of 20 things they thought could be improved with the SilkFred site.

I wasn't going to do that.

With so much riding on this, I wanted to go much, much further than a basic laundry list of SEO improvements. To do this, it meant exploring, auditing and investigating their site to a much deeper level.

That said, I did not have any special advantage. I used the typical SEO tools, like SEMRush, Screaming Frog and Google Search console, that everyone else had. I also had no access to special information, and what I gathered could be collected by any other applicant.

The difference I hoped would stand out was the level of work and detail. If everyone used the same tools to look at the same site, then the conclusions would likely be similar. By presenting a far more comprehensive report and plan, I intended to show my dedication and grab attention from the cluster of "same old" lists other applicants submitted.

So, I ran the site through test after test. I audited it using every tool I had. I collated a list with hundreds of SEO-related tasks and ideas I would love to do with their site. And I built a yearly plan and presentation to give all my findings and recommendations sharper context.

All up, it was over 20 hours of work, crammed in during late evenings and on a single day off.

But it worked.

By hitting them with the biggest audit they would have most likely ever seen, I scored an interview with them. The next hurdle: flying to London for the first time to convince them I was the perfect person for the job.

SECOND HURDLE: THE INTERVIEW

Being a small company, several people interviewed me, including the tech lead. This was another chance to stand out, as I could give him a tech-focused plan for SEO (i.e. a cut-down version of my Master Plan purely related to technical SEO).

The interview itself went well, and I got the chance to go through the detailed Gantt chart and plan I'd built for their site.

(As a bonus, this meant I had already finished most of the planning when I joined SilkFred!)

There was one moment that effectively won me the job. SilkFred's site at the time was heavily client side JS based, back when Google's ability to render it were slim to none. So, I showed them a blank page telling them "this is how Google sees your site right now". In other words, Google didn't see the JavaScript because SilkFred was blocking the resources. Just off the back of this explanation, they soon after unblocked the resources on their homepage, which was a quick fix.

When I showed them the blank page, there was silence in the room for several minutes... and not long after, they offered me the job.

4 TIPS TO BURST THROUGH THE DOOR

Let me go into the things I actively did to make the most of this opportunity.

Do the work

All up, I invested around 40 hours into the application process with SilkFred, including...

- Conducting the audit
- Further planning based on extra information provided
- Travel to and from London
- The interview itself

But I didn't mind at all. I was 100% focused towards getting the job, and spending this time was a great way of showing that to my employers-to-be.

Be generous

If you want a job as a senior SEO, a site audit is one way to show you will go above and beyond. But you may worry that if you give away too much, the company can use your report without hiring you. However, I think you should always look to do something like this for two reasons:

1. Highlighting potential problems is only half the story; they still need the "how to fix", which is where your real value lies.
2. When the stakes are high, you show you are more willing to put in extra work to set yourself apart from the crowd.

Seize the element of surprise

The element of surprise was an important factor in my hiring. SilkFred asked for a list of 20 items in the next three to four days. Instead, I went into overkill mode to give them a full-blown audit and report, all within that time limit. They weren't expecting the quality and scale I delivered, and it was one of the big reasons I secured an interview.

Get the techs on side

If you can talk with the techs early on — or even in the interview — that's perfect. You get the chance to show you sympathise with them and want to collaborate to improve the site at all levels. When I mentioned switching to server-side JavaScript to the lead tech, he whole-heartedly agreed and said he'd been saying the same thing. This set the scene for a great working relationship before I ever started, and added another feather to my cap during the interview.

A SHORT EPILOGUE

It is no spoiler to say I got the job.

The company had been so impressed by my audit and plan that not only did they offer me the position, they started implementing action items I had recommended. The result: a double-digit increase in traffic by the first day I walked through the door.

As the first in-house SEO specialist for SilkFred, it was a balancing act to build trust, advocate for SEO and secure the resources I needed. But now the company has seen the wins that come with SEO, I am confident the successes will nourish each other and let me achieve more and more.

THE SURVIVALIST'S GUIDE TO THE ENTERPRISE SEO JUNGLE

RICHARD NAZAREWICZ
TECHNICAL SEO MANAGER
THE WALL STREET JOURNAL

Richard has worked for over 15 years in technology and digital spaces, spanning various disciplines from technical consulting for high-end enterprise servers for Hewlett Packard/Compaq to a web developer specialising in SEO in the early days. He co-founded a Spanish-based digital agency focusing on the design and development of Websites, Web apps, and SEO. Today, he is the Technical SEO Manager for the Wall Street Journal.

Tackling SEO in any environment is a unique challenge. Handling it for one of the largest publications in the world is a different kind of "jungle" altogether.

I have spent decades in I.T. consulting and marketing, working on backend servers, as a developer, in my own agency, and of course, in the fascinating world of SEO. With my mix of skills and experience, arriving at the Wall Street Journal as an SEO Specialist was exciting.

Since then, I have thrived in the corporate SEO jungle thanks to techniques I picked up over my years of working in technology.

Today, I am going to share the best ones on how to survive the jungle yourself.

EMBRACE OPPORTUNITY

While some might have seen it as a challenge, I was thrilled to have the opportunity to work at the Journal. Of course, there are big differences between an SME and corporate environment, including:

- The sheer size of the website
- The global nature of operations
- Unfamiliar technologies
- So many new faces

But if you look at each more closely, you realise there are so many opportunities for personal and professional development. For example, I hadn't had as much experience working with Node.js/React, Agile, GitHub, or Jira before. I now know enough that I can audit and identify if there is something that is affecting SEO and Search Traffic, and then work with the developers and engineers to fix it.

BUILD YOUR OWN SITE MAP

The first thing I did at The Wall Street Journal was to sit down with a solutions architect and whiteboard the sitemap, navigation, and technology stack powering the various parts of WSJ.com. I took that raw image and built my own schema diagram or mind-map, which over the early days became a guiding star for me. I have since shared it with others onboarding to help them understand the complex architecture.

Each section of the WSJ.com site was mapped out: politics, business, news and so on. For each section, I noted specific details like:

- How was it built?
- What kinds of technology was it built on?
- Where was it located?
- Who was the lead engineer?
- Who was the product manager?
- What type of content was published there?

When grappling with a particular section, my "image sitemap" had everything I needed to know within a few seconds. These days, I don't tend to use it, but it was a virtual lifesaver in my first few months.

MEET AND GREET

When you talk SEO for any big news site, whether the New York Times, CNN or the WSJ, you can encounter the same or similar issues. The sheer scale means the sites have to work across multiple technology stacks and be managed by many teams.

Learning my way around the site was one thing. Getting to know the people behind each section was another. Within a few weeks, I was scheduling meetings with Product Managers, Engineers, Heads of Business Units, and others, all in the name of building my network. One of the most valuable tools in your SEO toolbox is your contacts, and that goes for external networks within the SEO community.

There are two things to remember when you do this in an enterprise environment:

1. In a company with offices around the world, you are not going to know everyone. Focus on those you are likely to have the most contact with, and then slowly expand your network as you settle into your role.

BEHIND THE PAYWALL

"How does Google index your site and rank it along with other content when it's behind a paywall?"

I hear this question a lot, even from SEOs, so I would like to set the record straight.

When we moved away from Google's "First Click Free" (FCF) paywall, The Journal — as did other subscription news sites — wanted to be in control of their own paywall and algorithm. So, we deployed an in-house paywall solution which has been highly acclaimed and has an amazing team constantly working to make the user experience and algorithm better.

Google understood that we and other publishers wanted their own paywall, and came up with a product called "Flexible Sampling" to enable publishers to use their own paywalls. Essentially, Flexible Sampling allows Google to crawl our full article text, index them, and treat them like any other non-paywalled page or article. You have to deploy some scripting and tags on your site to enable Flexible Sampling, but once done, Google is able to read and index an entire article page's content even when it sits behind a paywall and shows a non-subscriber only the article snippet you set in terms of word count.

2. Being a "people person" — even if you are an introvert — is possible. I am living proof an introvert/extrovert can make it work. Build a network of contacts and ensure you are able to find a way to work with even the most challenging members within any team or BU. It's sometimes very taxing and can seem like you will never succeed, but keep working on collaboration and always give praise when you do get help or cooperation, as it goes a long way. Remember times when you were praised for something you did or helped resolve; this is giving back that same feeling and making that person feel appreciated.

ORGANISE YOUR DAY

I am not sure how many truly master this, but organising yourself can be an important survival skill. Two things I do that help ease the day ahead are:

1. Use tools that simplify organising your day. I generally use Trello, which integrates with many other tools. I also use Mac Notes for the day-to-day, and never go anywhere without a notebook and pen: it might be "old school", but it still works.

2. Block out time in your calendar. I learned early on that if I needed something done, the best way to do it was to block out time in my calendar. So this is now a weekly ritual.

These are not 100% fool-proof methods, of course. Crises or sudden fire drills can derail your day. But if you're organised, you can keep the "workflow damage" to a minimum and get back on track faster.

AUDIT, ANALYSE, REPORT

A lot of people - including developers - see SEO as a dark art.

This is why reporting on SEO is critical. The best way to demonstrate the power of SEO is by producing results and reporting on them. Some of the principles I follow when reporting include:

- Make the reports informative…
- …but don't overload them, because people get lost in the data.
- Make them easily digestible.
- Keep it concise: nobody has the time to read a 20-page report!
- Label your metrics and data sources, as you may be asked or challenged on your findings and where they came from.
- Report your wins wherever possible, not just for management, but for your own record.

The typical metrics that go into reports are nothing special: Page Views / Visits / Uniques, Average Page Ranking, CTR, Pagespeed, Impressions, Clicks, Referrers, and Backlinks. To help show progress over both the short and long-term, I use rolling 14-day and 14-month average and totals in my reports.

NEVER STOP LEARNING

You might have heard the saying "sharpen the saw". In the corporate jungle, you don't have a choice. You have to keep the SEO saw razor-sharp, and that means research and learning.

You know firsthand that SEO is an always-evolving landscape. You have to keep your eye on it and stay on top of emerging innovations and developments. Personally, I love to use Twitter and listen to Podcasts during commutes to learn and stay in the know. You can also:

- Join SEO communities on social media like Facebook, Reddit or LinkedIn
- Follow some of the big SEO names on Twitter
- Watch a few of the great YouTube videos from Google Webmasters or other prominent authorities
- Subscribe to SEO Podcasts to listen on the go or when you have time (and take notes)
- Take the free certifications on Google Analytics or Data Studio

Beyond the online world, try to attend at least one to two of the big SEO conferences every year. It doesn't matter whether it is BrightonSEO, Pubcon, or Advanced Search Summit. Get out there and find out what people are talking about, so you are not caught out either. (This is also an excellent opportunity to practice your networking.) You might be asked to come back as a speaker next time, so always have a deck ready to show off your area of expertise.

Oh, and remember to share your newfound knowledge with others!

BUILD YOUR TOOLBOX

It's obvious to say "get the right tools", but that is often dictated by your budget. Most of these tools are not expensive, and make up some of my toolbox:

Screaming Frog
One of "the" tools us SEOs use, relatively cheap, and one of my favourites. If you work in a corporate environment, ask DevOps to work with you to install this on a cloud server so you don't have to run it locally on your

A TWITTER QUICK LIST

While there are hundreds of people you can follow on social media, these are some of the people and channels I follow on Twitter to keep on top of all things SEO.

- BERT: Dawn Anderson (@dawnieando)
- Googlers: Official Webmaster Channel (@googlewmc), John Mueller
- (@JohnMu), Gary Illes (@methode), Danny Sullivan
- (@dannysullivan and @searchliaison)
- Python, Data Science and SEO: Hamlet Baptista (@hamletbatista)
- Google Updates & SEO News: Barry Schwartz (@rustybrick)
- Google 360: Glen Gabe (@glenngabe)
- E.A.T.: Lily Ray (@lilyraynyc)
- SEO Futures: Bill Slawski (@bill_slawski)
- Technical SEO: Roger Motti (@martinibuster)

laptop or desktop. They also have a log analyser, which is not too expensive and relatively easy to use.

SEMRush

A relatively inexpensive tool we use for keyword research and competitor comparisons. For smaller sites, you can set up projects to audit your site and give you valuable information on site health, including a score that can be useful for reporting. They also have an API (though you have to pay for access) which allows you to export the organic research or project audit data into Google Sheets or Dashboard.Supermetrics

This is a connector that lets you connect many data points to Google Sheets, Data Studio, or Excel. I personally use it to pull data into Google Sheets and Data Studio and manipulate the data to build reports and dashboards as required.

Splunk

If possible, try to get access to or implement a log viewer like Splunk. If you have enormous logs but don't have a site-wide licence, you can dump the logs into an Amazon S3 bucket and have your DevOps people build a custom feed to pull into your reports.

Google Analytics

While Adobe Analytics is a solid option for Enterprise Analytics, Google Analytics is more collaborative. The way I compare the two is that Adobe Analytics is like Microsoft Office and Google Analytics is G-Suite: both are great, and some are better at specific functions than the other.

Google Search Console

This is a free tool that Google offers to allow you to submit your site to Google so that you can submit your sitemap(s), view raw search analytics (Google data), identify errors on your site, request indexing, and much more. They have an API to allow you to pull the analytics data into say Google Sheet or Data Studio using a native connector or using Supermetrics for better control on the granular data points.

Technical SEO Audit

I recommend using either Botify or Deepcrawl for an enterprise site, as they both allow you to crawl at high page-per-second rates over millions of pages. These tools give you great insights as to how Google may see your site and identify problems that you can work with engineering to resolve.

PROXIES, PRE-RENDERING AND PR: LESSONS FROM A BRIEF BRAND CAMPAIGN

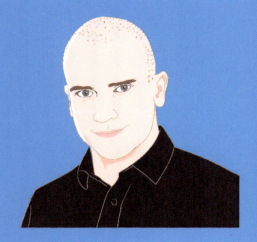

JAMIE PEACH

HEAD OF SEO EUROPE, SAMSUNG

Jamie's career in SEO extends back over a decade, after he got his start as an SEO Executive in Ladbrokes. Since then, he has acted in primarily leadership roles, including his present position as Head of SEO, Europe for Samsung. Jamie is also a speaker at numerous industry conferences, such as International Content Marketing Summit, BrightonSEO, SEO Barcamp and eTail Europe.

"You can't win them all."

The phrase is a cliché, but it is for a reason. Even the best of us cannot get everything right every time, especially when certain factors are against you. Consider this scenario:

1. Our company was about to launch a brand campaign that gave the SEO team little time to prepare.
2. I had joined the organisation only months earlier.
3. There were significant technical challenges.

It was far from a disaster, and the learning we took away has held us in good stead. Let me take you through three of the biggest takeaways.

ALARM BELLS RINGING

The brand campaign was for one of our flagship products.

The campaign involved a novel concept where the product was used in a way - and in an environment - few others could follow.

There was a lot of supporting PR and above-the-line marketing to drive demand as part of the campaign. Search's role was to be present when the expected demand appeared and reduce the reliance on paid advertising.

We brought on a big brand agency to help with the campaign. As is often the case, while they know what to do around brand, they don't have the same SEO nous. When they suggested using microsites and building the user experience with React, my alarm bells rang.

I had hoped we could work on our native platform to optimise SEO, but we hadn't factored the cost of building the assets on our site with the agency who maintained that. This was a major challenge, as we had two big technical issues on our hands:

1. How to handle pre-rendering for the app that was the focal point of the campaign

2. How to use our company's parent domain to help visibility

There was a third problem we were unaware of that would make successful SEO for the campaign even more difficult. For now, we focused on the technical tasks at hand.

> ## PRE-RENDERING: GIVING THE GOOGLEBOT A BETTER LOOK
>
> Pre-rendering is a method to preload all the elements on a web page so a crawler can read and index content without having to render JavaScript. This means dynamic Google (or other search engines) can index content or web apps more easily. There is often an equivalent version of the content included that a crawler can view without having to render.
>
> Pre-rendering is handled programmatically, so it takes development effort to build pre-rendering into an app or page. Given the short timeline and the fact our main site used a custom JavaScript framework (so we couldn't use our framework), trying to add pre-rendering into the brand campaign's React app would be almost impossible.

A PRE-RENDERING PROBLEM

React is a great choice if you want to build web apps fast. Many brand agencies use this library to minimise development time, which is a must when you deal with fast-moving campaigns. However, it is not great for SEO unless you have pre-rendering, and this agency used frameworks without pre-rendering. If it does not come with the framework, you won't have time to build and test it for a fast-moving brand campaign. Without pre-rendering, the odds are stacked against you that Google will read and index the site for it to be useful during a short-term campaign like this.

Not having that pre-rendering meant we weren't able to rank as we hoped. We did manage to apply it to a few pages involved in the campaign, like the landing page. But the web app — the centre-piece of this product-driven campaign — had no pre-rendering.

Because of this, important parts of our content weren't crawled. While we ranked for some of the main terms we wanted, longer-tail keywords were nowhere near the first page. This is where the lack of pre-rendering caused our SEO to underperform.

HOW A REVERSE PROXY WORKS

Simply put, reverse proxies control access to servers. When a client makes a request to a particular server, the reverse proxy intercepts it and behaves based on its configuration. They are typically used for purposes such as flexibility, performance or security.

In our context, a reverse proxy was a way to use our company's domain with the web app's site, even though the brand agency hosted it. We configured the reverse proxy in Akamai, setting up a rule in the DNS so the original address would redirect to the IP address we wanted.

LESSON: Get involved earlier in the agency selection process for upcoming campaigns, and have a say in who we work with to ensure their technical and SEO capability aligns with ours.

RECLAIMING OUR DOMAIN WITH REVERSE PROXY

Hosting the web app and associated pages somewhere else wasn't our preferred choice. But we had few options with the campaign fast approaching. So, I suggested a reverse proxy solution.

We had never done this before, so I had to investigate and draw up charts to illustrate how it worked. I also had to justify the SEO value, using examples of other sites. It seemed risky at first, as I uncovered several articles around a similar, somewhat controversial activity known as sub-domain leasing. With more digging, the team realised this wasn't related to our reverse proxy implementation, so we pressed ahead.

Again, this was not ideal, but we wanted to give the campaign pages domain authority and increased visibility, and the site's original domain would start from zero.

Our ability to get the reverse proxy up and running in time was perhaps our biggest win for the campaign. It was also a fantastic reflection of the company's culture. If you could get the right people to say "yes", things moved quickly.

LESSON: Don't be afraid to explore new solutions, even if they have never been done inside your organisation before.

WHEN PR JUMP THE GUN

Alongside the SEO and digital marketing for the campaign, we used PR agencies to build press momentum. This created an unexpected problem.

By the time the campaign went live (and in some cases even earlier), many of these agencies had issued self-congratulatory press releases that talked up their part in the campaign. The press releases took top ranking on Google for the keywords we had targeted, which stole visibility and diluted the effect of our SEO.

PR didn't come out of my budget, so it wasn't my responsibility. However, it had a direct bearing on what we worked on, so I flagged the problem with the campaign managers working with the agencies. Since then, we have set much clearer conditions in agreements around what agencies can release PR-wise without our approval.

LESSON: Set stronger conditions around what PR agencies can release, especially before and during a campaign.

SHORT-TERM CAMPAIGN, LONG-TERM LESSONS

Being a brand campaign, the main KPIs were very brand-led. Several of these measures included:

- Whether the campaign put our brand in a more positive light
- Whether the brand stood out more
- If the brand appeared more innovative

For all the effort and hype, the campaign was short-lived. The lessons we took away were not. It helped us identify technical limitations in partners we work with, handle process gaps with agencies that could impact rankings, and allow us to explore creative technical solutions with more confidence.

THE FAST AND FURIOUS: LIFE AS AN SEO EXPERT IN A START-UP

KERSTIN REICHERT

SEO DIGITAL MARKETING MANAGER, TIDE

Kerstin has been in digital marketing — and primarily SEO — for over a decade, in a career that has spanned four different countries. From SEO Director in Switzerland, Trainer in Austria and now SEO Marketing Manager in the UK, Kerstin has worked at both corporates and start-ups. She's a speaker at industry events and a member of IAB UK's Search Council, a body dedicated to educating professionals on better Search Marketing.

If I had to use one word to describe being an SEO specialist at a start-up, it would be fast. Luckily, I loved that kind of pace when I worked with agencies, so I am in my element at Tide.

But there were two other big advantages to a start-up compared to an agency. First, I get to own SEO end-to-end; something you rarely get to do working for clients.

Second, you are part of a larger marketing team, so you know what others are doing at any given moment. When you are working at an SEO agency at a client site, you can feel a little isolated.

This is a snapshot of how I navigated the early days at Tide as their first in-house SEO manager.

THE NOT-SO-GREAT OF START-UP SEO

When I joined Tide, a FinTech start-up in London, in January 2019, there had been little SEO work done.

In a way, it was refreshing. I was lucky enough to be the first to set the stage for the business's long-term SEO success. I still come in everyday excited by this. But like any start-up, you still deal with challenges and limitations, and SEO is no different.

The usual start-up constraints

While this is not the case any more at Tide, the term "start-up" can conjure images of people crammed together at a lunch table or CEOs sitting next to receptionists. Money and resources are tight, and you do your best with what you have got.

When it came to budget, I dealt with two challenges in the early days: a tighter budget than most non start-ups, and a near-obsessive focus on measurable, performance-driven activities to squeeze what I could from the money I had.

A blank slate

Yes, starting from next to no SEO was exciting, but it also had its challenges.

My early investigation showed Tide ranking for very few keywords because there was little content to rank. What ranked was mainly for long-tail keywords, and a lot of organic traffic came from our community pages. In one way, that was positive: it was user-generated content, and the language from our users was more natural than internal jargon. However, the traffic from this content wasn't ideal, as visitors landing through it often had a different intent than seriously considering our product.

The fierce competition

When you target small businesses in search engines, you have to be under no illusion about how competitive the battle for ranking is. For Tide, we were dealing with three kinds of competitors:

1. Established players in the finance field, like traditional banks
2. Other FinTech start-ups who offered similar products to ours
3. Anyone who focused on small business, like accountants

We couldn't disregard the third kind of competition, even though most were in different fields. From an SEO perspective, they were fighting for attention as we were, which made the situation that little more complex.

RAPID-FIRE RELATIONSHIP-BUILDING

There was another big obstacle to growing SEO in a greenfield environment: lack of awareness.

While the senior leadership understood SEO's importance, there wasn't as much consideration across the teams in the day-to-day. Many thought SEO could be done as a separate activity and without collaboration.

Educate others

When people think SEO happens by itself, they feel they don't have to be involved. So, from almost Day One, I was running with this message:

"we've got to work together on SEO, and this is why". I held workshops, got active in strategy meetings and played a part in planning, where C-levels attended. These all made an impact in improving SEO's visibility at Tide.

Network fast and furiously

To build a culture of SEO awareness, you have to network... but networking is different in a start-up. At larger companies, I struggled to get to the people I had to work with or convince them it was in their interest to invest in SEO. A start-up is smaller, so you end up knowing almost everyone. Here are a few things I did when building those relationships.

- Don't leave it too long before you connect with others. I had coffee catch-ups in the first week, while people were still interested in this newcomer.
- Try not to make the discussion about you. Avoid "Hi, I'm the new person, I'm going to do that, here's why I need your help" and so on.
- Instead, flip it around. Take time to learn about them, what their plans are and how you might help them.
- If you can network outside 1-on-1s, do it. At Tide, we have a lot of internal events, talks from different teams, team lunches and social gatherings.

Collaborate and cooperate

When projects appear on the radar where I need support from others, like a designer or developer, I am quick to put together a website working group. We have regular (but quick) meetings, put together our to-do-lists, and then work out priorities and resources from each department. This avoids those frustrating last-minute approaches not just for me, but fellow team members. It also means nothing gets missed, such as SEO considerations during planning for new feature launches and the campaigns that promote them.

This is not limited to working with individuals, but whole teams. For example, I work with the social media team when they have a big campaign on the horizon. I sit down with them and discuss the project to determine where I can help. This kind of collaboration yields much more from any initiative than if each team worked in isolation.

THE #1 LESSON LEARNED

When I started with Tide, I focused on SEO best practices over the first weeks. For me, this comprised three main areas: technical aspects of the website, content, and off-page partnerships.

But if I was to start again, I would lead with a product-first approach. SEO best practices are obviously important, but I would first take the time to understand our product teams and their roadmaps inside out before jumping into analysing the state of SEO or making any plans. This might seem obvious, but you would be surprised how often SEO professionals get over-excited at working on a new domain and launch straight into tech audits, when it would be more helpful to take a step back first.

I covered the customer side almost immediately, mainly by looking through the community pages and the questions they asked. I also worked with our support team to discover what they were getting contacted most often for. I wanted to understand our customers to better anticipate what they searched for. For example, we target a range of keyword categories along the conversion funnel.

KNOW WHAT CUSTOMERS WANT AND GIVE IT TO THEM

When we accurately predict what customers want, it doesn't just give us an SEO advantage. It sometimes results in new products Tide attracts new customers with.

For instance, we recently launched a product where you can both register your company and get a business current account for free through one easy sign-up journey. This understanding of a common customer problem — registering their business — helped us develop a solution to two big hurdles new businesses encounter.

I could see the search traffic around "how do you create a company" or "how do you register a company" and made content plans to address these. But by having a close relationship with the product team, I shared that understanding and worked with them to create this new offering.

1. **Upper-funnel keywords** that may not be as competitive. I think about other topics people starting a business or looking into it might search for and create content that covers this, and whatever else I can find along the customer journey.

2. **Lower-funnel keywords** where someone is ready to convert. They want to open an account for their business, so they search for "free business account", "business bank account" or other money-related terms.

Tide's mission is to make finance administration easier for small businesses and be their Number One financial resource. Ideally, people would find us while they are still considering a business or self-employment (i.e. long before they need an account). That is why the second type of keywords is important: it puts Tide in front of searchers early on and starts to build a relationship. It also helps us come up with new ideas that the product team might use.

UNLOCKING POTENTIAL

Life is still as fast and furious as the day I joined Tide. We have grown from around 80 people when I started to a company of over 350. When you are the SEO manager of a start-up, you deal with what gets thrown at you the best you can. These strategies helped me not just survive at Tide, but show the business the incredible potential well-harnessed SEO can deliver.

THE JOURNEY: WHAT TO FOCUS ON AS YOUR CAREER UNFOLDS

SAM ROBSON
DIRECTOR OF AUDIENCE, FUTURE

Sam has enjoyed a long career as one of the prominent SEOs in the media industry. Sam's first media role was as SEO Executive at Future, back in 2011. He later went on to be Head of SEO and then Head of Audience Development at Future. After spending a year in 2017 as Group Audience Development Director at Time Inc., Sam returned to Future, where he is currently the Director of Audience. He is now accountable for all Future's acquisition channels, including SEO, Social Media and PPC, with a team of 15 people based across Bath and New York.

Focus.

Every successful professional has it.

However, it takes more than focus to build a satisfying career. Focus is the HOW, but it is also WHAT you narrow in on that makes for success. And as your career develops, that focus changes. The things you do as a graduate are not the same things you do when you run an SEO team.

Here's what I focused on as my career unfolded.

STARTING OUT: PICK YOUR BATTLES AND PROVE YOUR WORTH

When you start out, pick which battles to fight.

It is tempting when you are new and enthusiastic to try a dozen different ideas. But you need to know which ideas will give you wins that prove your worth, and which — whilst maybe best practice — have less impact, and should be left for later. Prioritise the changes you believe will provide the biggest wins and prepare a solid case for them. Make sure you believe your own argument, and don't exaggerate potential benefits. Once you have proved you can deliver, you build trust with other teams and leadership and it gets easier to work with others. Once you have their trust, they will then help you deliver the best practice ideas you deprioritised earlier.

The best in-house SEOs have no trouble getting people to work with them. In many cases, it is the other way around: people want to align themselves with winners, and a good SEO willing to collaborate makes other teams more successful.

> ### HOW TO AVOID OVER-PROMISING
> One of the hardest things in SEO is knowing what impact a change will have. It is hard to model, so people will either just pluck a number out of the air or spend hours trying to model an

outcome without enough relevant data to do it accurately.

Be wary of over-promising. Avoid unqualified statements like "if we do this, traffic will go up 20%". But, this still leaves you with the problem of how to estimate the potential value of a project, which is a key part of prioritisation.

One way you can estimate is to use case studies from outside of your company. The SEO community is very helpful: people are happy to share their material. So, if you are not sure about what results a change might bring, try to find someone who has already done it. You can then present it as "whilst we can't be 100% sure on the benefit for us, this company saw a result of X% more traffic and I hope we'd see similar". It is an effective way to win people over to your side without having to guess or exaggerate.

KEY TAKEAWAY: Don't fight every battle. Be selective, and if you are going to make a push and ask others for help, make sure the potential can be delivered.

ESTABLISHED: COMMIT TO THE RIGHT THINGS LONG-TERM

Around five years ago, Future decided they wanted to become the biggest technology publisher in the United States. As a magazine publisher historically based in Bath, UK, it seemed ambitious, to say the least. But we had a clear strategy and a proven track record with existing sites, including TechRadar, which had been very successful in the UK.

With the vision set, we executed a strong SEO strategy. We weren't afraid to try new things. For example, we were one of the first publishers to implement hreflang tags back when they had just been released. Because it was so new, we couldn't find case studies, but it wasn't hard to argue we should execute the work because our strategy was so clear. We had our goal of becoming the top publisher in the US, and hreflang allowed us to tailor US and UK versions of the site to provide a better user experience. We later were showcased on Moz as the hreflang case study.

However, for the most part, our strategy didn't rely on cutting-edge techniques or anything revolutionary. We did simple things, such as hiring US writers to localise content and write US-first news stories whilst making sure the site was technically sound. Above all, we built our strategy around a user-first, keyword-based approach, and made the commitment to see it through. Execution is everything.

This is one of the big advantages of being an in-house SEO as opposed to agency side. Once you are established and have found the right company to work for, you can build for the future. If you get things right, they can pay off for the long-term, as they did for us. Things I did right on a site five years ago still benefit me today. Agency SEOs have to show results faster and rarely enjoy the luxury of working towards longer-term goals.

KEY TAKEAWAY: Develop your strategy, commit to it, and build for the future.

DOWN THE ROAD: INVENT NEW JOBS AND ADD STRINGS TO YOUR BOW

I became Head of SEO at Future in 2013. For some SEOs, this might seem as high as you can climb, however, I have been inventing new jobs to keep progressing my career. I have since been Head of Audience Development and then a Director at Time Inc. and Future. An interesting thing is that none of these roles existed before I filled them; they were created for me.

Director or Head of SEO is often seen as the ceiling in terms of a pure SEO role. To move beyond that, you need to take on new responsibilities. In my case, it made sense that if I was looking after SEO, I could also look after the other acquisition channels at Future. And over time, that is what happened: I took over Social Media, and then PPC.

Being able to do this stemmed back to my earlier days at Future, as I had the results on the board to show I could deliver consistently. I was also brave enough to ask for the added responsibilities, but there is no reason anyone with a good track record couldn't do the same.

There is a careful line to tread to ensure you take on new responsibilities in a way that is helpful for the company and without stepping on anyone's toes. But if you navigate that line correctly, you are in a strong position to succeed. Ultimately, any good employer wants their existing staff to deliver more as it makes your bosses' lives easier. If your company trusts you to deliver and you can offer them more, it's a win-win situation.

Of course, play it smart: don't ask for massive promotions or big salary increases before you have shown you can make the new job work. In a sense, you are starting out again and have to prove your worth, but if you work for a good company, trust that you will be rewarded once you have shown you have earned it. Good businesses aren't necessarily company-first or employee-first, you help *each other* succeed.

KEY TAKEAWAY: If you want to continue moving up the ladder, offer to pick up new responsibilities that complement your existing ones, so your job grows in stature organically.

MOVE JUST A FEW DEGREES

SEO doesn't work in a bubble. You have to collaborate with developers, editorial teams, or whoever. But when you do this, you have a choice: stay in your lane and focus on seo, or reach for opportunities that being across the business brings.

I liken this to moving just a few degrees away from what you do as an seo. The primary objective of seo is to bring traffic to your website through search results, but there are other ways people find and interact with a site. So, you may spot opportunities to help in other areas, like paid, social or even email.

You might branch out to get more involved with the content strategy, especially if the business is content-focused. This is why social media made sense for me: because a huge amount of what we do is content strategy, whilst seo or social are simply methods of distribution.

IT TAKES TIME

Just like training for a marathon, there is no easy or quick way to advance your SEO career. It takes time, dedication, effort, and focus. But if you work on the right things at the right time, you will develop into a better SEO expert and once you deliver consistent business results, there is no reason your career has to be limited to SEO if you don't want it to.

1. Pick your battles and prove your worth.
2. Commit to the right things long-term.
3. Offer to take on new jobs and keep adding new strings to your bow.

If you can prove that you can consistently deliver within your role, you have every chance to rise not just to the top of the SEO tree, but to build a rewarding career wherever you decide.

COLLABORATION AND COORDINATION: AN SEO MASTER LIST TO GET MORE DONE

RIC RODRIGUEZ
SEO CONSULTANT, YEXT

Ric Rodriguez is an experienced search marketing consultant with a history of working with internationally renowned brands. He currently works at Yext, a NYSE listed technology company, joining last year from iProspect, where he led a team driving organic search forward for clients that partnered with their sister media agency Carat. Prior to this, Ric held roles at well-known independent digital agencies, most notably within Croud and at Hearst's iCrossing. Ric has a genuine and infectious passion for marketing and technology and is a frequent author and speaker across well-known industry events and publications.

What do we mean when we say "collaboration"?

From an SEO perspective, we usually see collaboration as a way to network, build relationships, and then use those relationships when we need support. We talk about selling SEO to get more budget and resources so we can improve our organic standing and attract more traffic.

But when SEO (or any single channel, for that matter) becomes the priority above everything else, the business can suffer.

WHEN TWO TEAMS COLLIDE

As the SEO expert or leader for your company, one of your main responsibilities is to make sure the business thinks SEO. From a team perspective, this makes sense. However, the drive to push SEO — or CRO, or any one angle — can prove detrimental to the overarching business goals of higher revenue, more sign-ups, or better retention.

> ### SEO VS CRO: A SHORT CASE STUDY
>
> When I worked with an international brand, there was frequent discussion around how we should build landing pages for a number of their key services. These were critical pages for driving business enquiries, but at the same time, important for driving acquisition from search. The trouble was, the CRO recommendations were often at odds with the SEO recommendations — something I see in so many projects.
>
> The CRO team wanted less content, less information, and to drive people towards buttons (which made sense in the context of their objectives). SEO wanted more content and information, which would make buttons less distinctive on the page.
>
> Naturally, either side would have said their solution was best. In reality, it wasn't a choice of one or the other. I needed content on the page but it still had to convert reasonably well, since that was

> the whole point of the page. So, I chose a compromise solution. If the best case of the change was 100% value for each channel, I was willing to take 50% as a starting point — something is better than nothing — and improve over time.
>
> The senior stakeholders' priority was a return on their budget, and the intricacies of SEO or CRO operationally were something they were not involved with. For both teams to show value from the project, a collaborative compromise that delivered a percentage of what each aimed for was a sound decision. As it turned out, the pages drove a significant uplift that stakeholders were happy with.

THE TYPICAL WAY TO TACKLE SEO

In my experience, there seems to be a typical approach towards SEO.

First, you do some research and run audits on the site. You find out things like how many backlinks you have, how content is performing, if there are any technical issues, and so on. From that, you come up with a short list of tasks you need to do. Once you complete these, you look again, and find some new activities.

I don't believe this is the ideal way to approach SEO. You keep finding things to do, rather than looking at a site in any holistic sense. That means you approach other teams like developers or content writers constantly to ask for support. It is a non-collaborative approach: you take help when you can get it, but if a team doesn't have resources, it blocks you from completing a task. So, you look for the next one... and the cycle repeats.

COMPREHENSIVE, COLLABORATIVE SEO

One of the biggest differences I have made for businesses I've worked with, is to change their planning around SEO. While this approach encourages collaboration, it also helps SEOs look at their activities and goals strategically, rather than having to dig up tasks every few months. The process breaks down into four broad phases.

1. Research everything

The entire process typically took place over the course of a year - with the first phase centring around two months of discovery research. This research was far deeper than any audit. We gathered every scrap of data, dug deep into the structure of the site, and brainstormed fixes and improvements.

In the third month, we took the mass of data gathered and organised it into an itemised list that described, point by point, every single SEO task we could do. This ranged from massive, big picture projects to tiny fixes, like updating the internal links on a single page. In most cases, this ended up being a 500-600 point list. This wasn't a judgment on how little SEO had been done before (in most cases, the teams had already been carrying out great work), but a reflection on how much we had studied the site and the possibilities to improve.

> ## YOU MIGHT NEED SPECIALIST HELP... AND THAT'S OK
>
> To go deep, this research can often call for specific technical expertise. Since many in-house SEOs have to manage practically every aspect of SEO for their company, they tend to be more generalists. If that is the case, then I would recommend hiring external experts to help with this deep dive audit and research. This will not only give you greater insight into what is possible, but will free up more of your time to manage day-to-day work without being completely dragged into the research effort.

2. Score the list

The next step is as important as the research. You work your way through the list and score each item based on the impact you believe it will

have. It doesn't have to be complicated: high, medium or low is enough. Alongside the impact score, you also rate it for resource cost or difficulty to implement. For example, an item that needs both a front-end and database change gets rated far higher than an update to link text through the CMS.

Once finished, you have a Master List that gives you priorities, from quick wins to multi-month development efforts. It is with this list that you encourage collaboration with other areas of the business, starting with the next step.

3. Review the list

I sit down with three or four of the major teams impacted by our SEO list. That might mean the content team, development team, or CRO experts: anyone who may have a touch point with an item on the list. We then work through the list, re-rating each item based on their thoughts. This often proves enlightening, as a developer might look at a complex change I rated as high effort and advise it would only take half a day.

Getting a better assessment on the true effort required is only one aspect of the review. By sharing the list with these teams, I can ask when they are touching a certain part of the site and align a specific item with their plans. Together, we build a roadmap on what everyone believes is the easiest path with the highest impact, and schedule work around what is best for multiple teams.

4. Get it done

Once other teams understand the list and where it fits into their plans, you spend the rest of the cycle (usually a year) making it happen.

Now that you are in sync with other teams, more gets done. You rarely have to compete to get help, because both the SEO and development team know that in October, they'll deploy a change for Component X of the site. In November, the SEO and content teams will cooperate to update several cornerstone content pages, and so on.

When the last month of the cycle arrives, you review and evaluate your progress.

- Did you achieve what you thought you would?
- What will you prioritise for the following year?
- Are there areas you weren't aware of?
- Are there updates in other teams that affect your list?

Once you have conducted your review, the cycle starts fresh.

THE OTHER BIG BENEFITS

Collaboration is an important part and a big benefit of this process, but there is another business-wide benefit: transparency.

SEO is often seen as a less accessible skill or "the team always asking for help", neither of which is ideal for collaboration. With your list, everyone can see what you are doing, how it rates in terms of impact, and what is coming up. Plus, you have already aligned with other team plans, so you smooth the way instead of create conflict.

Another benefit your list brings is traceability and specificity. This appeals to most senior leadership figures, as they can see your exact plans and goals for the year. If you aim to tick off 30 items on your list over the next quarter, they have visibility on that. If you don't hit that goal, your review allows you to approach your manager for more budget with ready-made business cases.

IMPROVEMENT, ITEM BY ITEM

The first time I deployed this approach, we made massive headway into our SEO list: roughly about 30-40% of the items on their list within the first year. Essentially, it came down to knowing what tasks we could do, being aware of when other teams were making changes, and aligning SEO activities with them.

One of the master list's features I have yet to mention is the business continuity it provides once created. People can review the list to know immediately what is in progress and what is planned. This protects the business from long-term absences and makes it easy to onboard newcomers. The list also helps the business to forecast headcount to complete the tasks and budget accordingly.

Since that first instance, I have shared this method with several other businesses. Every time I take a quick look at their SEO (as we all do!) — usually via a casual check through a tool like SEMRush — they continue to improve and grow. And it is largely because the people I worked with continue to follow their Master List.

HISTORY AND LEGACY: JOINING A COMPANY AS THE FIRST IN-HOUSE SEO

ANGIE ROONEY
SEO PRODUCT LEAD, FINDMYPAST

Falling into SEO through a friend of a friend, Angie instantly gravitated to the creative and analytical mix SEO provided. Over her eight years in the field, she has worked as an SEO leader at several companies both agency and in-house. She is currently Findmypast's first in-house SEO specialist.

Trace a family's history back generation after generation, and you'll see how quickly it becomes complicated. But the twists and turns in a family tree have nothing on the SEO at Findmypast, the company I joined as their first in-house SEO specialist.

WHEN SEO IS SECONDARY

Findmypast has the largest online collection of British and Irish family records, which members use to search for their ancestors' records. These records can get very detailed; for example, I once read about my great grandfather and his wife judging a children's tennis tournament.

Findmypast previously outsourced much of their digital marketing to a media agency. The agency focused their efforts on PPC and display advertising, with a low level ongoing scope for SEO.

That all changed when two new people joined Findmypast: the Chief Revenue Officer and Head of Growth. Both coming from very online-centric businesses they were passionate about rectifying the historic underinvestment in SEO. They decided to bring SEO in-house and hire someone to lead it.

That someone turned out to be me.

HITTING THE SEO "RESET BUTTON"

Even before joining, I had a sense of what I might be getting into. During the interview, we discussed the previous challenges to implementing SEO and how best to embed a brand new position into existing ways of working. And when I asked about SEO tools, the reply was basically "Which tools would you like?". It was both a little nerve-racking and exciting to jump into this environment.

I've now been there for about nine months, and it has been a crazy, and at times overwhelming, experience. I have experimented, tested and learned a lot about hitting the "reset button" on SEO. These are five specific lessons I've come away with, being the first SEO specialist for a company that has never previously had this expertise in-house.

MAKE SURE KEY PEOPLE ARE ON YOUR SIDE

Before you jump into a situation where SEO has had little love, you want to make sure the right people will back you. To do that, you should find out the answers to these two questions:

A. How far does the belief in SEO extend in the organisational structure?

In an interview, you might only speak with your manager-to-be and one level higher. Finding out how far the belief in SEO extends, across ALL levels of the company hierarchy, helps you determine what kind of support you are likely to get.

If the CEO or senior managers have little faith, it becomes easy to prioritise other areas and leave SEO under-resourced.

If people at the execution level have doubts, you may encounter roadblocks when implementing.

B. When does the organisation expect a return on their SEO investment?

We all know that SEO can typically take a while to see significant results. But expectations might need to be managed, especially from those with limited SEO experience. So, in your interview, be sure to ask about their expected timeframes for results.

FOCUS ON THE FUTURE

When you are coming into a new environment where it hasn't always been plain sailing, blame is easy to do, but that is not a good approach.

When I joined Findmypast, unpicking the agency's SEO work to see what happened was fascinating. I did not point fingers, but looked for causes that would help me avoid a similar fate when implementing my approach.

It turned out that, because there hadn't been an in-house SEO specialist, the agency was flying blind. Without guidance or the feedback loop that's vital in an agency-client relationship, the agency experts delivered strategies and tactics that were never going to be successful.

One incident involving hreflang tags highlighted this lack of effective partnership. Our engineers had been instructed to add hreflang tags to our international websites... but there was a misunderstanding. Instead of adding four lines for each of our sites (and the x-default tag), the engineers only added lines for the other markets. So, our Australian site had no Australia tag, just the three for UK, US and Ireland. The agency's recommendation was implemented to the letter, and set in stone as the company-wide guidance - unfortunately it had missed a tiny, but crucial detail.

Obviously, this knowledge blind spot was not the engineers' fault. This is clearly something that an SEO specialist would know, but that cannot be expected from someone not experienced in the matter.

UNDERSTAND THE PAST

Whether there have been earlier attempts to do SEO or not, it is worth looking back to see what others have tried. In my situation, I found a folder named "SEO", which contained some of the documents from past agencies, filed into one place over a long period of time. However there was no structure, and even though I tried to go through the documents, many of them were out of date or lacking greater context. It was difficult to sift through the noise. So, I tried another approach.

I tracked down the people responsible for a certain project and asked them about it. They would recount what happened (or at least their version), which allowed me to get more of the story, especially around the who and the what.

Digging up the stories, rather than only relying on out-of-date documents lacking context, made piecing together the complete state of SEO at Findmypast more accurate. However, there were two problems I ran into while digging:

1. Some SEO tasks had been done over two years prior, and the people responsible had moved on. This left a lot of gaps in my understanding behind what had really happened.

2. Occasionally, I would stumble on something where team members had invested a lot of effort and energy, but not seen the SEO rewards, undermining their perception of SEO and motivation to work on future projects. My honest assessment of this touched a nerve, which led to another lesson...

ACKNOWLEDGE PAST EFFORTS

I was about four months in, when in a meeting an SEO project from two years prior was mentioned. I had never heard of the project, or even the part of the website where it existed.

Looking through the details, the project must have needed a huge investment in time and money. But like most of the earlier SEO efforts, the lack of successful client-agency collaboration meant much of the engineering team's work had been wasted.

It's been a delicate balance trying to evaluate a project that hadn't been executed correctly without stepping on toes. In all honesty, it meant an awkward, uncomfortable conversation with the engineers.

I found the best way to frame the conversation with those who invested the effort was to point out that this wasn't criticism of their work, and that we didn't want the time, money or energy to go to waste. By framing it constructively, we can move forward with the project so it delivers real SEO value to Findmypast.

ENCOURAGE OTHERS TO LEARN ABOUT SEO

SEO was clearly not on many radars when I joined Findmypast, but that didn't mean the interest wasn't there. Since my early days, I have been working to educate the entire business — finance, analytics, design, marketing, engineering, content and so on — about how SEO fits in. So far, the response and feedback have been extremely positive.

One of the most successful ways I have encouraged learning SEO is with a Slack channel. On "#Learn-SEO", I talk about SEO fundamentals in a way that's accessible to everyone.

Naturally, I want as many people to read the posts and learn from them, so I aim to make each post informal, entertaining and easy-to-read. This can mean:

- Using bullet points and emojis
- Keeping posts brief, with a link if anyone wants to find out more
- Including an occasional themed post, or finding relevance to our business

Here's an example:

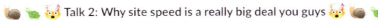 Talk 2: Why site speed is a really big deal you guys 🦌 🐌 🐢
- 53% of mobile users will abandon a page that takes longer than 3 seconds to loa
- A 1 second delay can cause a 7% reduction in conversions

More super fun site speed facts here: http://blog.kissmetrics.com/wp-content/uploads/2011/04/loading-time.pdf

MY FIVE TIPS TO FOLLOW

To be the first in-house SEO specialist and start from scratch is a challenge. To be the first in-house SEO and have to "reset" ineffective efforts, undo work, and start over, is tougher again. Fortunately, I have an amazing boss. She, and her manager, move heaven and earth to give me the support required to get Findmypast's SEO firing on all cylinders.

But at the end of the day, it comes down to me. And while I have learned much more than these five, they stand out as lessons anyone starting SEO in a company would do well to follow.

1. **Make sure key people are on your side**
2. **Focus on the Future**
3. **Understand the past**
4. **Acknowledge past efforts**
5. **Encourage others to learn about SEO**

SELLING SEO: HOW TO GET A BIGGER BUDGET TO GROW ORGANIC AND YOUR CAREER

ELI SCHWARTZ

FORMER DIRECTOR OF GROWTH & SEO, SURVEYMONKEY

Fascinated by how affiliates used SEO to generate traffic and leads for one of his early employers, Eli moved into the world of organic and growth and never looked back. Having spent over a decade in-house driving successful growth and SEO programs, Eli now works as an independent consultant, helping clients such as Mixpanel, Fishbowl, Getaround, Quora, Shutterstock, and Insight Timer. He also speaks at marketing events throughout the US, Europe and Asia.

I was fortunate to have landed the Head of Global SEO job at SurveyMonkey.

At the time, it was one of the largest brands on the Internet, but had never formally done SEO.

In my first week, I made an SEO recommendation for a massive change about to go live. The response from one of the chief officers: it was the stupidest idea they had ever heard.

Though I was already an expert in SEO, that moment taught me one of my most important lessons on the subject. It is arguably more important to understand how to sell SEO than any other skill.

THE GREATEST CHALLENGE IN SEO?

One of the biggest challenges to working in or leading an SEO team is that it is rarely at the top of a company's priority list. When an SEO leader sits to discuss budgets, goals and priorities, they often get overshadowed by the "glamourous" Paid Advertising team. After all, the bigger the budget, the more important that teams seem to be.

Naturally, the discussion revolves around ROI and revenue. And there is no doubt that paid advertising is an important piece of the revenue puzzle; it has to be when a business spends millions a month on it. But often, companies spend more on paid marketing than they earn, confident that a future influx of customers and sales will justify the investment down the track.

On the other hand, SEO is valued in an almost opposite way. If you ask for budget when starting from zero, any increase seems unreasonably high. After all, even a modest investment of £50,000 (which pales in comparison to most paid budgets) seems ridiculous. Even if you are able to secure some kind of funding, you then have to deal with expectations of near-instant results.

PAID AND ORGANIC: SAME SIDE, SAME COIN

As you will soon read, I position Paid and Organic as opposite sides of the coins when I pitch for budget. In reality, they are both on the same side of the same coin, working together.

Take life insurance as an example. Very few people instantly convert because they clicked on an ad and you scared them into buying. Instead, ads might convert prospects already familiar with you, but introducing them to your brand is where Organic shines. If they first came across your ranking article "15 reasons why you need life insurance right now", they get introduced to your brand. Two weeks later, they recognise your brand ad and click through.

I saw it myself at SurveyMonkey. It was hard to justify ad spend on long-tail keywords, so the majority of spend was on brand. The critical cog moving people towards brand search was Organic, and when we conducted multi-touch attribution, we found that in many cases, the first touch was Organic.

A BETTER WAY TO SELL SEO

When it comes time to set goals and determine budgets, it is important that you, as an SEO Leader, have a "seat at that table". If SEO is not represented, then it — and the SEO team — usually get scant attention.

Getting a seat at the table is only half the battle. You need to be able to fight for your team, and the best way to do this is with two methods I use to get the funding and attention Organic deserves.

Contrast

If I'm sitting next to the Paid team leader, it is easy to contrast budget requests. They might be managing a two-million pound budget, while I am asking for a paltry £50,000 for an Organic campaign. I will also point out to the executives that, unlike Paid, I am aiming to return 10 times the investment over the next five years without needing further funding for the campaign.

When I get that funding, I typically follow this model to bring in those kinds of returns:

1. Create high-quality content.
2. Develop a link-building campaign around the content.
3. Rank for a key term or topic.
4. Leave it alone.

Every sale as a result of that content lowers the average cost of conversions, since you don't have to keep spending, like paid campaigns. Once you've generated £50,000 revenue, you have hit break-even. At £100,000, you have doubled it.

Alignment

The second method to get a louder voice at the table is alignment. I encourage any and every SEO manager to align with a team doing something similar, but spending much more money. Again, Paid is a great example. They get much larger budgets, and money is constantly flowing into the team.

When you align with a team like this, you can say you are doing much the same thing. For example, when it comes to search ads, both teams target the same users. The only difference is that one user might be "lazy" and click on an ad instead of an organic result. If you show alignment, it highlights that your budget is far more moderate, even though you serve a similar function in the business.

THE #1 ORGANIC MEASURE TO AIM FOR

As a consultant, I work with companies in different industries. One of the big things I teach each is that rankings are the worst metric to use for measuring SEO. That's because rankings don't belong to you, they belong to Google.

Instead, I measure the success of an Organic campaign the way a business does: the revenue, leads or customers that turn up as a result. This also changes the conversation at the table. You no longer pitch "I need funding to hit this specific keyword", but "I need funding because I believe there is a revenue opportunity". This is a stronger business argument, and one executives understand.

What's more, when you achieve that revenue target, you strengthen your position to make another ask. Even if you fall short by 10%, you have brought in a solid return for the company.

BUILDING A BETTER SEO CAREER

So, what does all this have to do with building a career in SEO you can be happy with?

I believe few companies understand the real value their SEO team delivers, which means salaries and careers pale in comparison to the "high flyers" in paid advertising. And that ultimately comes back to one thing.

Promotions, raises, bigger responsibilities all come when you show the value of SEO to your business. If you don't have a seat at the table and don't contribute, nobody cares (or even knows) about you, your team… or your career. When you successfully secure budget — and show the results you can achieve with that money — you start to get noticed. Your value skyrockets, which opens doors for your career.

To return to SurveyMonkey, I know that a vast majority of all conversions came from Organic. When you think of their $250+ million annual revenue, with most of that coming from SEO, that is a lot of value generated by the team of 5 or 6 people that I managed. When you can highlight those kinds of results, you don't just get a better seat at the table, you get to say "Look at what we have done with so little budget… now, let's talk about my career".

WHY SEO IS MORE THAN SEO

DOMINIK SCHWARZ

CHIEF INBOUND OFFICER, HOMETOGO

Dominik began his career in online marketing back in the early days of 2005. It was here he discovered SEO, and soon became a specialist in the field. He now leads HomeToGo's Inbound Marketing team, where it won the best in-house team award at the 2019 UK Search Awards. Before HomeToGo, he was Director SEO Europe for the travel search engine KAYAK. Dominik is also the founder of Vertical Inhouse, an organisation that provides resources especially for in-house SEOs.

The SEO industry has a mixed reputation for good reason.

For the past ten years, we have fostered the image of SEO as something magical and mysterious. The rare few who mastered this skill were seen as Google Whisperers, conjuring Position 1 (or even Position 0) rankings with a wave of their wands.

This image ultimately hurt a lot of SEOs, both in-house and agency-side. As you know, SEO is nothing like this.

So, what is it?

Over the past 12 years, I have formed my own thoughts on the topic. These are 6 elements around what I think SEO really is.

SEO IS... HARD TO DO

Before anything else, let's acknowledge that in-house SEO is difficult to do.

It is not activating a couple of plug-ins, running a basic link-building campaign, or managing a project for a week or two.

SEO is complex, and something we need to work on constantly. That is why we have in-house SEOs. If you are new to a role or SEO is new to the company you work with, it is important that this gets acknowledged by people outside your team.

Of course, proclaiming SEO a tricky business to everyone you meet is not the best way to go about it. You need management understanding and support from the other teams. This is so important, especially as you may have to manage misguided expectations that SEO is something just "switched on" or something that works immediately.

SEO IS... MORE THAN A SPECIFIC SKILL

In this era of the ever-evolving Google algorithm, manipulation is no longer a game anyone can play. SEO rankings get measured on the experience our website gives a user when they click through.

So, what makes a high-quality experience? Amongst others:

- Copy that gives users what they want
- A great product that provides a solution
- Navigation and UX that makes the site easy to use
- Page design that enhances the tone

All of these deliver a better experience, which leads to better visibility and SEO. Yet, if you approached your manager to ask for a copywriter, designer or developer, you would be likely to get rejected. You might even be told to "just do SEO".

That is why C-level or senior management buy-in is critical. If you don't have support, it is impossible to move the needle far without design, interface, product or messaging, no matter how well you "do SEO".

SEO IS... PART OF SOMETHING BIGGER

This might sound controversial, but I don't believe there are many SEO-centric KPIs.

Most of them are ultimately business or people KPIs. We might push for better rankings, but that is to drive traffic and increase conversions, whether they are sign-ups, purchases or something else.

Take higher dwell time, for instance. We don't know if a higher dwell time increases your SEO rating, as far as Google is concerned. But perhaps the more important question is: do we care if it does? If we are able to get the right people onto the right part of our site and encourage them to take the right action, then I want a higher dwell time whether it makes a difference to my rankings or not.

SEO IS... NOT SOMETHING YOU COPY

It is easy to look at more successful competitors or markets and think if only we can emulate their SEO practices, we will enjoy similar success.

For example, if I worked on an e-commerce store, I might eye Amazon enviously and try to copy their SEO strategy. It would most likely backfire, without me ever really knowing why.

The reason is simple: **each business is in their own unique space**. Your business is not Amazon or whoever the market leader in your space is. Plus, you will never fully understand their strategies looking outside in. You might glean a few things, but will likely go down the wrong road, and waste a lot of time doing so.

At the companies I worked for, we always built our plan according to what we thought most important. We wanted the best content for visitors to increase engagement, keep them around longer, and develop some kind of relationship with the brand... and that is something you simply cannot copy.

SEO IS... SOMETHING YOU CAN TRUST OTHERS WITH

In my experience, organising jobs, skills or responsibilities in the typical team set-up often creates silos that stifle collaboration and communication.

It is one reason why HomeToGo created 360 degree jobs. If you're the country manager for Great Britain, you are responsible for inbound marketing in this specific market. You are not just the SEO expert, but the marketing and context expert too. In the course of your work, you…

- set out the content strategy for the country;
- find the right stories for the right destinations;
- create those stories and content;
- maintain contact with the media;
- take care of SEO,

I believe these rich, diverse jobs are the type to attract the best candidates, which is why HomeToGo doesn't recruit pure link builders or other super-niched roles. Of course, SEO has a specialist element: it is why you are an in-house SEO. But we can (and should) trust others to handle much of the non-technical, non-specialist work that is still vital to SEO.

SEO… TAKES TIME

We all know the hardest part of in-house SEO is starting at the beginning. But you don't just need buy-in and support. Both you and the stakeholders need patience.

Building the infrastructure and setting up how to create and scale SEO and content across multiple markets was one of my first big challenges after arriving at HomeToGo. It was a great deal of front and back-end work where we (naturally) didn't see any results for months.

It is when things take time that your planning will be tested. If you believe in what you have, you have to back that planning and carry it through. SEO success doesn't come from a Word document full of great ideas.

This comes full circle as to why you need the backing of your management. If they understand you need time to put the infrastructure in place, you can focus on getting that done. If they have unrealistic expectations and what rankings within a few months, that creates a problem for you. Even the fastest set-up will take weeks at best — weeks where you do nothing to visibly improve SEO — so managing expectations is a fundamental part of SEO.

THE IN-HOUSE SEO MANIFEST

These are a few of the things that make up what SEO really is. However, there is a more important and relevant question to answer:

What is the difference between those who are successful with SEO and those who struggle? I thought about this frequently, and it led to the creation of the in-house SEO manifest. These 21 principles are the distillation of what I have seen over my 12 years in the field.

Read through each principle. Let them sink in. And may they help you on your journey as an in-house SEO.

Printable PDF:

bit.ly/2Q9Mpaf

THE INHOUSE SEO MANIFEST

INHOUSE SEO IS **HARD.** IT'S NOT A DEPARTMENT, NOT A PLUGIN, BUT A PROCESS THROUGHOUT THE WHOLE ORGANIZATION. INFORM. **PERSUADE.** INHOUSE SEO IS EDUCATE. ENTHUSIASM FOR QUALITY, CURIOSITY ABOUT THE NEW AND PERSISTENCE IN EXECUTION. CONVINCE YOUR MANAGER. **EXPLORE. CREATE.** THEN THEIR MANAGER. **TEST, FAIL, LEARN** THEN EVERYONE ELSE. **AND REPEAT.** INHOUSE SEO IS TEAMWORK. **IT ONLY COUNTS IF IT'S RELEASED.** THERE IS NEVER A LACK OF RESOURCES, ONLY WRONG PRIORITIES. **START MEASURING TODAY.** KNOW ALL YOUR FIGURES BY HEART. INHOUSE SEO IS **KNOW** WHAT CAN BE STRUCTURE AND OUTSOURCED **PLANNING. AND WHICH TASKS CAN'T.** BUILD THE BEST POSSIBLE PRODUCT FOR YOUR USERS, NOT FOR YOURSELF. BUILD THE BEST POSSIBLE TEAM. BE PATIENT - GOOD RESULTS CREATE VALUE. SPARK JOY. TAKE TIME, BETTER RESULTS **EARN MORE LINKS. TAKE MORE TIME.** CONNECT WITH FELLOW INHOUSE SEOS SHARE, LEARN AND **DO NOT BELIEVE GROW. RANK. SEARCH ENGINES. QUESTION THIS POSTER.**

VERTICAL INHOUSE

IMPOSTER SYNDROME AND SEO: BEATING BACK SPECTERS OF SELF-DOUBT

TRISTRAM DE SILVA
TECHNICAL SEO MANAGER, TICKETMASTER

Tristram has been in the SEO field since the early days of 2006. Over that time, he has worked with The Digital Property Group in a senior SEO role, consulted across the fashion, health, travel and retail industries, and more recently for LiveNation, one of the largest live entertainment companies in the world. Tristram has been with Ticketmaster for over seven years and is currently their Technical SEO Manager.

It can happen to anyone — 85% of adults have experienced it at some time.

Nobody is safe from it.

I've dealt with it myself from time to time.

What I am talking about is imposter syndrome, and my experience with it as an SEO professional.

IMPOSTER SYNDROME IN SEO

Imposter syndrome is common in every professional arena. As mental health and wellbeing becomes more widely discussed, more people are speaking out than ever before. However, the triggers for imposter syndrome within SEO may arise for different reasons than in other professions, perhaps more so as in-house SEO. I personally have found a few triggers and remedies along the way.

Lack of Team Interaction

Over the years I've worked solo, within SEO teams and as part of multi-disciplined teams. I'm lucky to have worked with and alongside some very talented people over the years, and each of them has influenced my perception of SEO in one way or other.

But whilst the autonomy and freedom that comes with being a solo SEO is certainly something to be cherished, not having daily interaction with other SEO professionals can have a negative impact.

If you presented a scenario to multiple SEOs and asked them to formulate their recommendations, you would get as many different responses as there are respondents. That's because so much of SEO is about your personal experience and because SEO is so expansive, there's immense value in tapping into the experience of others when planning and problem solving.

I've always found myself to be more effective when I could turn around and bounce ideas off other SEOs sitting around me. As a solo player you don't have that luxury. There've been times when this led me to question my ability to make robust and effective recommendations. There's a bit more pressure on the solo player because the thinking, decision and direction start and end with you.

And when you feel you are second-guessing yourself, you can lose confidence.

Lack of opportunity to learn

SEO is an exciting industry; it's fast-paced and full of smart people who are constantly pushing the boundaries. Not a week goes by when you don't read something interesting, clever, and innovative. Whether it be a white paper or write-up of an interesting experiment, often these things are so far out of reach to an in-house SEO that you can but dream of being able to spend your time on stuff like that.

When the day-to-day reality is a near-perpetual cycle of firefighting and same old same old, rather than implementing innovative SEO practices and pushing boundaries, you can begin to doubt yourself after a time, given how fast the industry moves.

Should the chance ever arise, are you capable of deploying SEO campaigns that can realise their fullest potential? Perhaps you're not as effective as you could and should be? And if so; just how ineffective are you? Perhaps you're missing something obvious? When other SEOs look at your sites are they cringing?

Lack of resources

I've spoken with many other in-house SEOs, and I often hear the same thing: struggling with limited resources and buy-in. This touches me personally. Ticketmaster is an energetic and dynamic business, we're in strong growth, and we're in the midst of a large replatforming project. Securing development resources in the face of stiff competition from other areas of the business is a constant struggle. It is easy to become demotivated when you are unable to get even the simplest, glaringly obvious, quick wins into production.

At various points over the years I've often found myself wondering when someone would question what I had achieved in my position. Fortunately, I developed several ways of beating back the specter of in-house SEO imposter syndrome.

BUILD RELATIONSHIPS

It's been one of the hottest topics for in-house SEO training for a while now, and rightly so. Relationships are central to success in SEO.

I have long been an advocate of building solid rapport with others, especially those who unwittingly control some of the SEO levers.

There are obvious roles like product managers, developers, UX & UI designers, web editors, content writers and of course, marketeers. But I've had some of my best successes when working with some of the less obvious roles. Roles like PPC & Programmatic, Distributed Commerce, QA, Systems Engineers, Tech Operations.

Also, people in 'upstream' roles who make decisions which can influence how a website is populated can have an impact on how effective you are as an SEO. These can be roles like account managers, Sales and Partnerships. Moreover, if you're in an industry where you push a lot of content or inventory out to affiliates, partners & white label sites then connect with the people who control how that content is disseminated – mainly those responsible for APIs.

Effectiveness imparts confidence, so explore the business and develop relationships.

When I work with colleagues in other departments, there are three things I generally do out of courtesy, but which also build rapport so next time I need some help, I'm more likely to get a response and a friendly one at that!

Appreciate the effort of others

When someone helps you out, that is time they lose for their own work.

Acknowledging this goes a long way, as workplaces seem littered with rude people who don't show gratitude. Most people don't care about SEO, and they often don't have to help you, so when they go out of their way, I always show my appreciation.

Share results

Another fantastic way to deepen relationships is to show the time they took to help has had a positive effect on the business. The most important thing is taking time to share the results. I've found formats not too important; it might be as simple a screenshot of some results or as in-depth as a case study or automated report. So long as you can clearly show the effect of your colleague's help, that's the main thing. Always include a TL;DR - that's another tip!

Educate

I don't mean to teach SEO basics (though that never hurts). I mean to highlight to others how SEO impacts the business and how they can do their bit.

A few years ago, I worked with an engineering team in Gothenburg who did all the work on a platform serving the majority of our international markets, but wasn't getting the buy-in I needed. I identified that most of the engineers didn't understand SEO too much – to them it sounded like a lot of complex work for no apparent reason.

Shortly afterwards, I flew over to meet the team, showcase the effects of their work, and demonstrate that the platform's SEO health wasn't great. It took several days, but it paid off. Once the team and I reviewed the site in detail, they were more receptive to helping and began enthusiastically picking up SEO work from the backlog.

RUN YOUR OWN EXPERIMENTS

It is not always possible, but another way to escape imposter syndrome and rebuild confidence is to put effort into peripheral sites rather than the main sites.

For a number of years we've had sites on WordPress. It started out as just blogs but that has changed over time, the number of non-editorial sites increasing steadily. The great thing about these sites is they're external to the main Ticketmaster sites. The design and dev resource does not sit centrally, we have a great deal more agility with these sites. We're not constrained by the backlog and blockages that we have on our primary sites.

Over time, we have used the sites to learn and experiment, and to prove the value of SEO to the wider business. The success of the sites has been hard for the business to ignore. We're pushing boundaries and driving great results.

Our biggest success to-date has been driving 3,000% traffic increase year-on-year to a particular site. Almost all others are in strong double-digit growth. Not only are we now seeing a major shift in perception of - and investment in - SEO, we're able to take those learnings to bear on the SEO initiatives we are implementing on our core websites.

Of course, none of this would be possible without exceptionally skilled colleagues and the rapport we have built with them!

GO 'OFF PISTE' TO KEEP YOUR SKILLS SHARP

The monotony of routine SEO can allow imposter syndrome to creep up on you. The best antidote is to mix things up and do something different. To break out of my rut, I looked over friends' websites for free. This worked well for several reasons.

- You have the chance to explore and learn new verticals.
- You get to dust off the basics which you so infrequently get to use in-house.
- You can run small experiments quickly and safely.
- You reduce the frustration or isolation of being an in-house SEO.
- You get to learn what works for smaller sites where it's often harder to succeed.
- You take these learnings into the day job, regaining confidence and being more successful.
- Your friends owe you one!

Plus, you can work in a much more agile way, which is not always the case when you are in a corporate environment.

GUIDE OTHERS

Once you've explored the business, you should have a fairly good idea of which roles can improve SEO. Enthuse them and create best practice guides they can follow.

Most of the time it's very simple changes to the way that they work. Set up reports for them. Give them the tools they need to demonstrate success to their managers, who will, as a result, become your allies in advocating SEO best practices. It's reassuring to see the positive effects from these initiatives, and it also presents opportunities for case studies which you can use to engage and enthuse colleagues in other roles!

All the time you're learning and feeling like you're being productive, which helps you fight off imposterism.

FIND COMMUNITY

The SEO community is amazing, but nobody is 100% correct or a one-person encyclopedia, which makes a network to share ideas so important. There is a collective benefit to discussing your thoughts and hearing other opinions. So, whether you jump on social media or attend a conference, get involved in the SEO community.

(Note from Simon Schnieders: We invite you to join Blue Array's monthly meetups in London or Reading. The London meetup is the capital's largest monthly SEO event, and we ensure the conversation flows with free beer and pizza. Find out more at www.londonseomeetup.com)

INFLUENCE THE MEASURES OF PERFORMANCE

This can be very effective when it comes to changing mindsets and opening opportunities for SEO traction internally. When it comes to organic search, the metrics & KPIs reported up to senior management are often only the widely understood metrics or those which facilitate direct comparison to other channels.

As such, these reports tend to be more traffic & conversion focused. I've found this can lead a business to evaluate organic traffic and allocate resources based on what hits the site rather than what's required to get the traffic in the first place.

Showing the value of raw metrics like clicks or impressions goes beyond the traditional (and flawed) 'where did we rank' question. It helps the business understand that SEO is as much what happens in the search engine results pages as what happens once that traffic reaches our sites. We know the value of a click or impression for each page type on our site, and for the common phrases used for our content. It can sometimes help to show the value of users in each of your channels. Perhaps the return rate or propensity to purchase is higher with organic search visitors than it is with other channels who enjoy higher investment and support.

At Ticketmaster, we go one step beyond the norm and raw metrics like these are an important sub-layer of SEO performance measurement.

* * *

How you deal with imposter syndrome may be different to how I did it. Every person can find their own ways to boost confidence and push back the ghosts of self-doubt. But however you tackle imposter syndrome, never forget you're the SEO expert at your business and that you should not feel out of place.

LIFE IN THE NEWSROOM: SEO IN THE "BREAKING NEWS" LANDSCAPE

CARLY STEVEN

HEAD OF SEO (THE SUN), NEWS UK

Carly is an SEO veteran of the digital media industry, having worked in the field for over ten years. The Daily Mail was her introduction to both SEO and the newsroom, and she has been drawn to both ever since. After her time at The Mail, she served as a consultant for The Montreal Gazette, worked for City AM, and is now the Head of SEO for The Sun.

30 November 2015.

That was the day The Sun dropped its paywall and made content free to read for everyone. Readership rose, but the publication wanted to push its audience as high as they could online.

That is why they now needed SEO, and why they hired me.

INTRODUCTION TO THE NEWSROOM

My career as a newsroom SEO started years earlier and at a different publication, The Daily Mail. I wasn't there to work on SEO, but somehow ended up being asked to introduce SEO into the newsroom.

If I had known how intimidating a newsroom packed with journalists and editors can be, I would have declined. Plus, nobody really knew what to do with SEO back in 2008; there was no job description and few guidelines. So, I focused on the essentials, like optimising headlines for keywords.

Newsroom SEO is a little different to traditional SEO. We optimise for the Top Stories section of Google News, rather than organic results. When we first started, only a select few publishers could appear in the Google News results. But because it was brand new, doing basic SEO best practice paid off quickly for the team at the Mail.

By the time I started at The Sun in 2016, SEO — and my mission — was very different. My goals were:

1. Establish an SEO team.
2. Grow search traffic for The Sun.
3. Build a loyal, engaged audience.

To achieve those goals, we have tried many things. These are five of the more important takeaways uncovered over the past few years.

UNDERSTAND YOUR AUDIENCE

This is the key to everything we do.

Fortunately, The Sun has a clear picture of who our audience is. We have an audience team who analyses everything the publication does, so we know what our big traffic drivers are. For example, Love Island drives a huge amount of traffic to The Sun site. That means we actively cover it and make sure that content ranks well.

Naturally, this goes beyond SEO optimisation. Much of our success comes down to content quality, and this is where other departments shine. Our TV & Showbiz department is key to this, as they have plenty of industry contacts and score regular exclusives, which help drive performance. When you know your audiences, you can feed them a constant diet of high-quality content they want.

USE FORMATS PEOPLE WANT

When you understand your audience, you learn not just the content they want, but the format they prefer. These are two that were particularly useful for SEO.

Explainers

You have probably searched for things like "when is easter in 2020?" or "is brexit happening?" at some point on Google. Today, you see results that directly answer your query, but years ago, that content didn't really exist. Part of my mission when I started at The Sun was to explore the potential of these question-based searches. We came up with explainer articles written especially to target that traffic. Since then, this approach has become popular and most news publications produce this content too, so the playing field is far more competitive than it once was.

Live blogging

Live blogging is something we are trying to integrate into our processes, as we see immense value in it.

It is clear people want real-time updates, and not just for live sporting events. Plus, Google loves this style of content: live blogs tend to rank well in big breaking news situations. We need to work hard to convince editors that dedicating a reporter to a single blog for a whole day when they could be producing multiple separate articles is worth the sacrifice.

At the height of coronavirus search interest, we were able to carve a space for ourselves in the Top Stories rail with our live blog. Its fantastic performance is a big deal for us, as it helps make the case for future live blogs.

TICK BASIC BOXES

This is something I learned back at The Daily Mail. Once we found our feet, we worked closely with reporters and editors to ensure content was SEO-friendly. We created a best practice guide, and had SEO team members tweak headlines and make other small changes. It was fairly basic on-page SEO, but it paid big dividends.

A newsroom's pace is frenetic, and even today it can be a challenge to get reporters to follow standard SEO process all the time. It is not that they are reluctant to use SEO; they have seen screenshots that illustrate the difference SEO makes. However, editors can push reporters to move onto their next article, so SEO optimisation gets overlooked.

Today, we are much more sophisticated. We are not just thinking about how to rank for keywords, but how to increase click through for our stories. This might mean tweaking how the headline looks on mobile or what images appear in the Top Stories rail. We obsess over these details in a way that didn't occur to us in the early days of 2008.

THINK LONG-TERM LOYALTY

Building long-term loyalty is not something you typically associate with SEO, but it has become an ongoing part of our work.

SEO brings in a good part of The Sun's traffic, and we don't deviate from maximising that. However, with our larger team size, we have been able to dedicate time to investigate how we keep readers on the site and convert

them to loyal, engaged readers.

This means not just reaching as many people as possible, but as many of the RIGHT people as possible. For instance, a good percentage of our articles focus on soap operas. This is because we know readers who enjoy this content are more loyal and often return to the site. They generate far more value for us than someone who googles "when is mother's day", finds the answer on one of our pages, then never comes back.

Loyalty is tricky for search: people google what they want, find their answer, and leave. Loyalty is not a priority. To be honest, how our SEO team not just reaches people, but gets them to engage and build loyalty with The Sun brand is still a work-in-progress. That said, we have one way of building loyalty baked into how we work...

BUILD YOUR BRAND WITH OTHERS

Our eventual aim is for visitors to become committed readers of The Sun. However, that rarely happens after one or two visits; it takes at least a handful of return visits to build that loyalty. Luckily, we have help from other brands to keep people coming back for more.

As a publication, we are very TV-focused, which is a broad niche. Shows like Love Island and EastEnders drive a lot of traffic for us. By leveraging these subjects — or brands — we build a relationship with readers and eventually convince them to make The Sun their go-to news site.

If the numbers look good, we make the effort to add other brands to our stable. Strictly Come Dancing is a great example of this. A few years ago, we barely ranked for it and conceded the show search-wise to the BBC and others. But we realised the potential it had to draw readers, so we invested heavily: writing about it, getting exclusives, and giving the show frequent coverage. It eventually paid off, and we now have another well-ranking avenue for readers to find and engage us with.

NEVER STOP LEARNING

I have loved every minute of my return to the newsroom. You live for the big stories and moments; when a major story breaks, you are in the middle of the action. Even the pace of an average day is fast, and the stories always change. One moment you might work on breaking news, the next ever-green content.

Over the first year of my time at The Sun, we enjoyed phenomenal growth and bedded down the SEO team. Over the following few years, we learned a great deal on how SEO supports news in today's search landscape. However, I know there is more we have to discover, and I cannot wait to learn about it myself.

THE NEED FOR SPEED: SIMPLE PAGE SPEED OPTIMISATIONS TO MAKE YOUR SITE FASTER

ROXANA STINGU
HEAD OF SEO, ALAMY

Since 2006, Roxana has immersed herself in the world of digital marketing. Most of that has been in SEO roles, where she has specialised in technical SEO. Roxana is now the Head of SEO at Alamy, an online photo agency for stock, video and live news. She also speaks on SEO at conferences such as Brighton SEO.

We all know the part that page speed plays in SEO.

But how many of us actually dig into pages stuffed with CSS, JavaScript and other resources to give our sites a decent speed boost?

For some, this is a daunting topic they would rather not touch. This article is here to not only "demystify" page speed, but to give you some simple techniques to clean up things that slow your site down.

THE PROBLEM WITH REPORTS

When you talk about speed, the first thing to dive into… is not reports.

Sure, they are useful and can indicate where issues lie. The problem is that they only provide a "what's right or wrong" with your site. They never tell you how to improve things, so a lot of the time, that improvement never happens.

As one example, Lighthouse lets you run audits with a couple of mouse clicks in your Chrome browser. When it generates a report, it tells you there is JavaScript blocking rendering of the page.

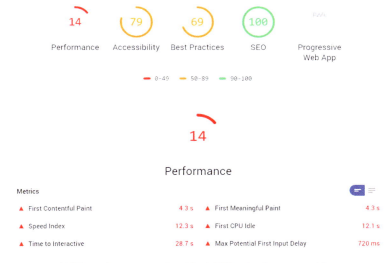

Lighthouse is an easy way to get basic SEO and performance metrics on your website… but it doesn't tell you how to address problems.

But because many SEOs don't know how to fix the "what" that reports show, it tends to mystify technical SEO and make it seem harder than it is.

Generic recommendations serve a purpose, but it's not hard to go much further. If you have a site you're looking to speed up, you can start with nothing more than a web browser.

NOTE: this isn't always practical for agency folk, as they don't get the time to get into lower-level details. If you're an in-house SEO, then you probably do have time to dig deeper and help deliver these kinds of wins to your company.

SYNTHETIC SPEED VS PERCEIVED SPEED

Just like report results often do not tell the full story of your site, machine page load times from a tool are different from perceived page load times. In most cases, machine speed is less important for one reason: users don't care if your page load times hits benchmarks. If it takes too long to "load" (i.e. display above-the-fold content they can interact with), they simply leave.

In other words, we have to adopt a "user first, technology second" approach. Rather than run audits and tests that satisfy arbitrary targets, we have to look at sites the same way our users do and optimise the experience for them.

BROWSER TOOLS + PATIENCE = PAGE SPEED WINS

Once you understand what you are searching for, it is reasonably simple to identify page speed improvements for your site. All you need are the Google Chrome Devtools and a little patience to make sense of what you're looking at.

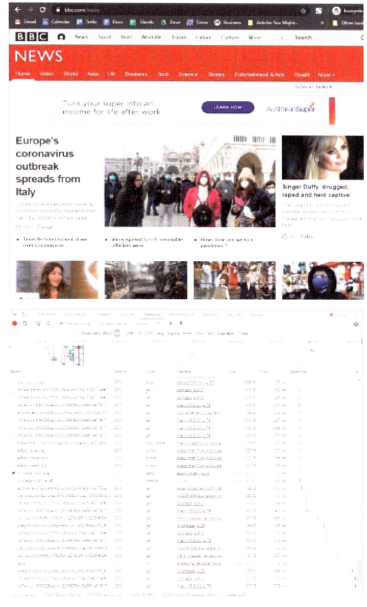

Observing which resources are fetched - and in what order - when your website loads gives you a treasure trove of potential speed fixes

Push back scripts

Scripts are prime culprits in blowing out load times. To stop them blocking a page render, there are two HTML tags that push scripts back in the loading process and let the rest of the page load more quickly.

Async

When a page's HTML is parsed, it fetches any script in the header and then executes it. This temporarily stops parsing and extends the page load time. Applying the *async* tag to a script indicates that parsing can continue while the script is fetched. Only once the script has downloaded will parsing stop to execute, which allows more of the page to load in the meantime.

Defer

The *defer* tag is a little different to *async*. Instead of just fetching a script in parallel like *async*, *defer* won't execute the script until the HTML has been fully parsed, letting even more of the page load.

One thing to watch: test these tags to ensure nothing on the page is inadvertently broken by delaying script execution.

Break up large files

If *async* or *defer* tags can't do the job, there's a more "heavy duty" option. Large script files that eat up time while they download may be broken into separate files: a smaller part with page-critical scripts to run early in the parsing, and non-critical scripts to load at the end.

(Of course, your developers can slice up script files beyond this simple divide, so discuss with them if you're exploring this route.)

The Chrome Devtools, under the "Coverage" tab will show the CSS and JS scripts used on the page, how big each of those files are, and how long they take to load. This is a solid starting point to track down bigger files that slow page loads.

Optimise images

Images can be very quick wins in the speed stakes. Compression is a basic step, but they should be resized to be no bigger than the maximum size they're used at. Many images get loaded at sizes exponentially larger than what they appear as: a 1000x500 logo that displays at 250x125 is a great example.

Something to note: resizing via HTML *img* parameters does nothing to improve results from image optimisation, so make sure you resize actual images.

Watch third party resources

Watch the Network tab while your site loads and you won't miss the amount of third-party resources that are part of your page. These resources include:

> ## IT TAKES A TEAM TO BUILD SEO
>
> When my team works with the developers, marketing, or any team in the company, we try to win them over by putting numbers behind any task or project. This can mean things like number of pages impacted, in both worst and best case scenarios.
>
> When an SEO initiative comes close to the best case mark (or exceeds it), we make sure everybody involved knows, so they're proud of what they helped accomplish. In fact, we don't call these "SEO wins", because they really weren't. As SEOs, we cannot achieve much on our own. It takes a team effort to make a difference.

- Tracking (such as Facebook)
- Analytics
- Advertising
- Tag management
- On-page tools, like chat clients

Since these come from sources beyond your site, it is hard to control their speed. But you can control how soon they load. This is one of the reasons Google cares about above-the-fold content and not full page load. Third party resources don't affect content, but do affect page load times. So, if you can push these resources (or any not needed in the above-the-fold) further along the loading process, you speed things up for the user and satisfy Google.

Another issue to check is whether a certain resource needs to load at all. Third party resources often hang around long after their usefulness has ended, adding to the page load time for no reason. Tracking down why a resource is on the page (and whether it should stay) takes some work, but removing unused resources can lead to extra performance dividends.

THE PROOF IS IN THE PAGE SPEED

We implemented these measures on two template pages of Alamy's site, then tracked the results. The templates were used by about 170 million other pages, so we had plenty of data to observe.

The improvement on our image pages' load time averaged at around 20%. In actual SEO value, this translated to an 8.3% increase in sessions and an 8.9% increase in users over the next 30 days.

I want to reiterate that unlocking these page speed improvements wasn't difficult to do. Any in-house SEO with enough time could do the same. You don't need advanced coding skills; just a Chrome browser, a basic understanding of what to look for, and time to speak with experts in other teams.

SCIENTIFIC SEO: A TEST-DRIVEN APPROACH TO VALIDATING SEO

FELIX WELCKENBACH
FREELANCE SEO CONSULTANT

Felix has worked in Search for over a decade, starting his career in SEO for an online dating agency in Hamburg. Over the years, he has worked in several industries, culminating in a Senior Manager role for an enterprise company in the travel industry in London. Recently, Felix launched his own consultancy to work with corporate clients to improve their SEO and digital marketing.

A/B testing might not be on the list of things you think about for SEO.

From my experience, I haven't seen many companies that do scalable A/B testing for their SEO. It often was the province of enterprise-level companies, such as the travel site I worked for — but it does not have to be.

This type of testing may not be for everyone, as the complexity may make it prohibitive for some smaller businesses. For us, it proved to be a scientific, measurable way to validate whether our efforts around SEO made any difference. It also helped to frame conversations about investments into product and resources with leadership teams and stakeholders.

WHEN BEST PRACTICE ISN'T BEST

Like many disciplines, SEO has a lot of best practices you can follow. In one sense, this is good: you can use these fundamentals and often score some easy wins from them. But when you have covered the SEO basics, best practices are no longer much good.

Another issue is context. Any SEO technique, best practice or otherwise, may work well for one business, industry or market and fail in another. To understand whether something really drives value, you have to measure it. Implementing site features without gauging the impact (positive or negative) means you are flying blind.

When you add site features you know have measurable value, even if it is small, you can show the compounding effect of your SEO initiatives over the short, medium and long-term.

That is a key I believe for SEO in every business, even though it is not common practice yet from what I have seen. Of course, there are good reasons most companies have not explored A/B testing for SEO.

THE CHALLENGES OF SEO A/B TESTING

These are four obstacles I have seen with SEO A/B testing that might prevent wider adoption:

1. You need a certain traffic level to run tests. If you don't have enough incoming sessions, it is hard to achieve statistical significance that returns an accurate result. You could spend months running a test without getting conclusive results which makes the exercise ineffective.

2. A/B testing requires certain knowledge and skillsets in-house if you want to build and maintain it for yourself or even just onboard an existing solution. Giants like Booking.com or Amazon would have their own models and processes, but they have the resources to create and maintain these. For many smaller businesses, this outlay is a big entry barrier. However, there are third-party solutions out there you can get started on and make this practice available to many more companies!

3. As I touched on, the SEO industry still relies heavily on best practices. SEOs focus on implementation but often don't take the time to measure the results of their work beyond the implementation phase. This can be very costly, as the compound effect also works in the opposite direction, harming your business results by productising a non-beneficial feature or website change.

4. Many content management systems don't make it easy to make the desired changes to a template or page type without Engineering resources in order to create a variant version for testing.

While these challenges make A/B testing difficult, the benefit of being able to validate and measure the impact of your SEO initiatives is invaluable, and something I recommend any SEO at least investigates.

THE KEY A/B TESTING COMPONENTS

There were two main components

The Testing Framework

Instead of building our own solution, the tool we chose was ODN, an SEO split-testing platform offered by an agency called Distilled. It provided all the functionality necessary to run and evaluate an A/B test for SEO including:

- Automated bucketing of similar pages into control and variant groups
- A meta CMS framework to make the necessary changes to your site
- A mathematical model to measure and evaluate the results
- In some cases, the ability to rolling out the change after a successful test

The Process

Having chosen the framework, we then built an operational process around it. We based our approach on the Scrum methodology popular

with software development teams in order to create an agile environment, enabling us to react to market and landscape changes very quickly.

In true Scrum style, we ran fortnightly sprints where we would take the top idea from our prioritised backlog of hypotheses and test it. Once the test achieved a statistically significant result, we assessed the results and decided whether to productise it. We then moved onto the next idea.

We improved the process over time, which accelerated our test velocity and helped us understand more quickly what worked and what didn't. Something else to consider for prioritisation are opportunity costs: The smaller the change you make, the smaller the potential business impact (in theory). As you block a certain group of pages to be included in another, potentially more impactful test, this can become quite costly. You can only run so many tests in a year. Be bold!

SEO A/B TESTING IN ACTION

Here is a quick example of how we typically conducted an SEO A/B test.

1. We select a certain type of landing page (for instance, those based around cities) and bucket them based on similar user behaviour and traffic levels into two buckets:

- Control: an unchanged version of the page
- Variant: where we make a change, like extra content

2. We then turn on the test, wait for Google to crawl and index the changes (important!) and then let it run. How long it takes depends on the volume of traffic and the magnitude of change.

3. Once the test has accumulated enough traffic in order for the test to reach statistical significance, we review the results. The metric we care about most here is organic traffic.

There are several blog articles about the mechanics of split testing but in short, bucket testing analyzes organic search traffic to the test pages in comparison to the control group. In particular, the difference between the forecasted traffic for the control group and the actual traffic of the variant pages in order to decide if a change was beneficial or not including a predicted uplift in traffic.

PUTTING THE SCIENCE INTO SEO

By applying a scientific approach to SEO, we were able to measure the impact of any site feature we thought might be beneficial. A/B testing allowed us to evaluate our ideas for both organic traffic and conversion rate, which gave us a quantifiable and compelling case and helped with prioritisation. This helped us secure resources and advance the cause of SEO with engineers, C-level executives and other stakeholders. Overall, split testing improved the perception of SEO all throughout the company.

During my time at the company, we ran around 10 to 15 tests a year. This does not sound like much, but it was a big step from zero SEO split tests the years before. The overall uplift achieved from implementing successful test ideas was between 5 and 10% in traffic and revenue. As we improve our testing process and keep velocity up, results will compound over time, delivering long-term growth for the channel and the company, and giving SEO a greater voice and influence.

THE SEO SCALE: HOW TO TELL IF YOUR NEXT COMPANY MEASURES UP

ADAM WHITTLES
HEAD OF SEO, AUTO TRADER

Websites and custom-built PCs were Adam's introduction to technology, and he discovered SEO soon after. He freelanced for several years, then started his agency career in 2012 with Ayima Search Marketing. After stints at two other agencies, Adam moved in-house to become an SEO Program Manager with Apple. Currently, he is the Head of SEO for AutoTrader, one of the UK's most visible sites.

When I started learning SEO, black hat techniques were normal.

This was around 15 years ago. Google wasn't as dominant and there were other search engine options. People shared their tactics about what worked with Google in online forums — such as Digital Point, WebmasterWorld, Warrior Forum, SEOMoz Forum, and Black Hat world — which is how I got into SEO.

It wasn't until I decided to make a career out of SEO I realised how much more there was to it. I joined an agency to learn the intricacies of SEO, and for the next several years, worked agency side to round out my experience.

Finally, I made the jump to in-house SEO. I had worked with Apple in my agency days, but joining them in-house showed the incredible differences working on the other side of the fence.

AGENCY NOW, IN-HOUSE LATER

It wasn't until I went in-house that I appreciated the value of agency experience. I had worked across many industries and clients, and have seen the challenges each one faced with SEO. It prepared me for in-house, even though I dealt with all-new challenges.

When you go in-house, you learn that company's challenges down to the finest detail. It sharpens your skills in certain ways as you grow and adapt to meet those issues. However, you can get sucked into the company bubble, whereas with agencies you keep being exposed to more situations, people, and clients.

I compare this to learning from textbooks. You could read one textbook over and over to become an expert on one niche. But if you don't read other textbooks on other subjects, you won't develop well-rounded knowledge.

This is why I recommend junior SEOs or people starting in the field to work with agencies first. Once you have that broad experience, you are better equipped to go in-house and drill down into specific areas.

SEO IN THE ORGANISATIONAL DNA

When the time is right for you to explore in-house opportunities, you realise how different those opportunities can be. It comes back to one critical factor: how well an organisation has embedded SEO into their DNA.

While you might spot many clues, these are four things to look for when assessing how SEO-friendly an organisation might be:

1. The general priority of SEO

Can you tell where SEO fits into a company's plans? Can they show they have invested in SEO previously? Through conversation, you can get a sense of how much importance an organisation puts on SEO.

2. The size of the SEO team

The company's size often dictates this, and some don't need huge teams. At AutoTrader, we run a very lean operation of only three. However, the size of the team can be one measure of how the business sees SEO.

3. Tools and techniques used

Tools and techniques are another way to gauge how seriously they treat SEO. Simple, cheap tools don't automatically show an organisation takes SEO lightly, but if they have invested in sophisticated tools or use more advanced techniques, that is a promising sign.

4. Support available for SEO

To get things done as an SEO, you need developer resources. If you don't have that, it is difficult to achieve much. Will the organisation give you that kind of support?

Naturally, not every company you look at will score 10/10 on an "SEO scale" that indicates how well-embedded SEO is. That is not necessarily the problem. However, if you are considering working with a company at a lower level - a 1 or 2/10, or even a 5/10 - there are things to be aware of.

1 OR 2/10: FROM THE GROUND UP

You may not see many of these for a good reason. The reality is a company that scores a 1 or 2/10 on the SEO scale is unlikely to have a dedicated SEO or be searching for one. In those cases, you will probably never join any organisation in this state.

However, if you are a broader marketing expert who has an SEO background, you might come across these companies. They may hire a digital marketer, with SEO being one of a dozen responsibilities they have to handle. SEO is clearly not embedded in their DNA, and even a specialist would struggle in these circumstances.

There is a rare scenario you might consider. A company may score 1 or 2/10 for SEO, but realise its importance and want to prioritise the channel. So, they hunt for an SEO Lead. I have interviewed at companies where they don't get SEO but want an SEO person. My advice would still be to think

START-UPS: AN EXCEPTION TO THIS RULE

Start-ups can be an exception to the "score low, avoid" rule, and I have seen this happen frequently.

Regardless of whether they are 100% online, they can focus on branding and marketing but not realise how important SEO is. Once they grow to a certain size and realise the reliance they have on organic traffic for revenue, they adjust their priorities and give SEO and their website the attention it deserves.

These kinds of businesses can be great opportunities for in-house SEOs. If the company is willing to invest significant resources, you can be confident of being able to move them from a 1 or 2/10 on the scale to an 8 or 9/10.

hard about this, and ask plenty of questions. You need to be sure they are serious about SEO and willing to invest in it beyond 1 or 2 hires.

A DIFFERENT KIND OF WORK: 5 OR 6/10

Joining a company that has already embedded SEO to some extent doesn't mean you avoid problems.

You may not have to fight to get tools. Stakeholders will probably listen to your advice on SEO fundamentals. Your battleground will be around influence.

Connections and relationships are your most important assets when you work in-house. At an organisation that sits around 5 or 6/10 on the SEO scale, that counts for double. You need other teams and stakeholders to achieve SEO success, but that does not mean they will line up to help.

When I joined AutoTrader, there had already been investment into SEO, but it wasn't necessarily one of the key business priorities. The first thing I did was to learn what the situation was: where opportunities lay, what challenges faced us, and what other teams were doing. From that, I created our SEO strategy.

The secret was not in creating that strategy, but selling it. I went on an internal roadshow to get buy-in from senior leadership and other teams. Having that strategy helped sell the journey, but it was the act of presenting, talking with others and building relationships that proved key. After a couple of months, SEO became a priority and resources like developer support helped us to build momentum.

ALMOST SEO UTOPIA: 9 OR 10/10

When I arrived at Apple, SEO was embedded to a degree I have rarely seen. For example, product teams had checklists whenever they launched a new page, product or campaign, with one of the first things being to talk with the SEO team. We also had a large team of dedicated SEO developers available.

This outcome results from a level of maturity the business has reached with their SEO over time. It is a natural part of their DNA, is understood across the entire business, and getting support as an in-house SEO has much less resistance.

Should you have the chance to work at an organisation like this, I highly recommend it. You can focus on implementation with less worry about politics or budgets. You get the chance to experiment or work with advanced strategies, so staying up-to-date with the SEO world is important.

Note: building influence and relationships still applies at places like these, though you probably won't have to work as hard to do so.

* * *

The SEO scale is not infallible. Sometimes it will be hard to judge whether a company is a 1, 5 or 8/10. What is important is that when you make the leap from agency to in-house that you scrutinise the organisation. When you find a business ready to invest in SEO, you know you will make a bigger difference not just for your new employer, but for your career as well.

CROSS-CACHE: WHEN PAGES "JUMPED" COUNTRIES (AND HOW I FIXED IT)

EMIRHAN YASDIMAN

**TECHNICAL SEO LEAD,
METRO MARKETS GMBH**

A LinkedIn ad asking for trainees turned out to be Emirhan's introduction to SEO. He rapidly rose up the ranks, leading his first SEO team after 18 months. Since then, Emirhan has led SEO efforts for agencies and organisations in Turkey and Germany.

If you're not familiar with the phrase, "down the garden path" means to mislead someone.

In 2018, I worked for a hotel aggregator site. When we looked into the caching of some of our international sites, we realised that Google was sending many of our visitors "down the garden path".

A PERPLEXING PROBLEM

The first sign of a problem was the cached version.

If you looked up the cached version of our Canadian site, you might end up on the UK site. Google struggled to pick the difference between sites that shared languages, and had started "cross caching" them (as we called the problem). That meant our Canadian site got traffic from the UK or even Australia, and vice versa.

We sat down to investigate the problem, only to find it even more confusing. To simplify the sheer volume of hreflang tags we had to deal with, we set them up in the sitemaps for each site. However, Google acted like the tags didn't exist, which showed that Google wasn't reading our sitemaps any more.

On the surface, the problem may not have seemed too serious. But there were complications.

One was that the vendors we worked with varied from country to country. So an Australian user on the Canadian site would see different options than on their native site, which could cause problems or prevent the user from being able to book. Other country-specific options — like Germany's EC Karte — would also not work if you were on the incorrect country site.

A TALE OF TWO TAGS

When we checked the server logs, we confirmed that Google had been fetching our sitemaps less and less. Even after I changed something manually, Google refused to fetch them.

With the *hreflang* tags embedded in the sitemaps, we thought about the obvious solution: moving the tags into each site's code. But with 65 versions of our site — 1 for each language / locale pair we supported — it was too much effort even to automate. We compromised by adding the tags to the home page and city pages for each site.

This was a partial solution, but it didn't stop individual hotel pages "jumping" from one country to another. When I looked in Google Search Console, I could still see a myriad of errors with international targeting.

We kept digging to get to the root of the problem. Each domain had around two to three million hotels against it. For those that shared the same language, the only difference was the hreflang tags, which were no longer working.

WHICH HOTELS IN WHICH COUNTRY?

We used an automated system to check if a hotel record was relevant to the country site it sat under. The two to three million hotels in our systems were copied across those 65 language / locale pairs, so we needed a way to minimise unnecessary duplication.

On the first day of every month, the system would look at every hotel's activity over the past 365 days, and across each of the 65 versions of the site. If a hotel got at least one click in a particular country, it was indexed under that site. If it had gotten no clicks in the past year on a country's site, the system would determine that hotel to be irrelevant for the country and apply a *noindex* tag.

Unfortunately, the system worked independently on each site. There was no way the system could look at our database and not index a hotel in Russia because it got no bookings there. We had to find a better way.

Obviously, hotels could be popular in some countries and get no attention in others. Our existing approach applied noindex tags to hotel pages in countries that had no conversions in the past year. To illustrate, if you were traveling from the UK to Turkey, you might only book a hotel in a major city like Istanbul or Ankara. Being outside of Turkey, the thousands of local hotels would be of no interest. That being the case, we didn't want those smaller hotels indexed beyond the Turkish site. To manage this, we used a system that checked hotel records and added noindex tags to those that were not relevant to a certain country.

I checked the indexation of several pages, and found that records with a *noindex* tag were not getting removed from the *hreflang* tags. That meant the instructions we sent to ignore hotels were in turn being ignored by Google.

STARTING FROM SCRATCH

Because the *noindex* tags were at the heart of the problem, we decided to scrap the system we had and start again. This would be a big investment, so we wanted to prove what we were planning would work. I volunteered

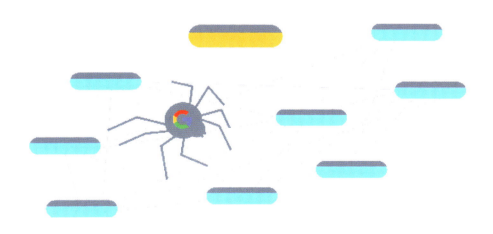

to conduct a manual "test run" on four sites experiencing the problem: Australia, UK, Canada and Ireland.

I got someone from the Business Intelligence team to sit with me, and over three days we recreated the sitemaps from scratch. We didn't need much, just the CSV files for each site that had:

- The hotel ID for each record
- An index / noindex status
- The number of conversions for that record

If conversions were greater than zero, the hotel was indexable and went into the country's sitemap.

The first country to have a new sitemap uploaded was Ireland, as they were the lowest risk. After Ireland, Canada, Australia and the UK soon followed. We then watched and waited. After two weeks, I could see international targeting errors dropping across those sites. Traffic is always volatile in travel, so it was hard to confirm whether the fix had helped in that respect. On the technical side, everything looked good.

That was only step one, but it was enough to prove the concept and secure budget for developer time.

The second step was to recreate the hreflang tags based on the now correct index statuses of the hotels. Once a sitemap was updated, the system would check where else the hotel was "live" conversion-wise, and only add the hreflang tags where that was the case.

The developers built the automated system over 10-12 weeks, following on from my investigation and manual work. It took two to three weeks after release to fix the issue across the board. All 65 domains were now correctly tagged, and hotel records would only appear under sites where they had conversions.

This episode was not catastrophic for the hotel aggregator. It didn't cause massive revenue loss or traffic to plummet. But, it was a timely reminder that technical SEO is a complicated creature, and having in-house expertise to investigate hidden problems was a resource worth investing in.

WHY YOUR SEO RECOMMENDATIONS DON'T GET IMPLEMENTED

(and what to do about it)

BEN HOWE
SEO Manager at Blue Array

As an SEO, I'm fascinated at how often stakeholders invest in our services, give regular affirming feedback, but fail to implement recommendations when it comes to the crunch.

Sometimes the void between feedback & end product feels totally irrational.

I experience this as part of an agency (where our stakeholders are clients) but I've seen in-house SEOs experience this with close-by functions.

At Blue Array, we go to lengths in prospecting to illustrate what resources clients need to succeed. We outline that every prospect will need:

- a percentage of regular development resource;
- a marketing executive (or equivalent).

New clients accept these terms, but implementation remains a problem for me. I feel equipped to react to it, but not everybody is. Not everyone is inclined to.

Many of us are secretly OK with non-implementation. We don't have to mop up sloppy details. We move to the next exciting idea, and shed responsibility for progress.

But if stakeholders aren't implementing, the accountability is ultimately ours. With my skill set, I'll only be a radically successful SEO if I see this coming, account for it, and head it off before it hinders progress.

To solve this, I surveyed 51 SEOs for experiences of non-implementation; and researched whether biases could be affecting decisions.

I'm not qualified in psychology or behavioural economics, and a perceptions survey with 51 respondents is never going to win awards for data science.

But it all helped me identify common seemingly irrational non-implementation scenarios, biases that account for them and actionable tactics to offset them.

This essay looks at the three most striking findings. But first, the survey details.

THE SURVEY

I surveyed 51 SEOs in a perceptions-based survey:

- Blue Array account handlers;
- Blue Array alumni;
- A few SEOs from social media.

The focus was tightly on seemingly irrational non-implementation. Broader reasons for SEO failure have been covered by indomitable SEOs including Aleyda Solis (Search "What makes your SEO fail").

In brief, the survey covered:

1. Are we getting the basics right? Do we generally have an agreed, specific, time-bound plan?
2. Can we read into the effects of seniority on implementation?
3. Are there common non-implementation scenarios?
4. Enthusiasm vs implementation: are there any key turning points in a client or stakeholder lifecycle?
5. Are there common actions we particularly struggle to get implemented?

This generated a lot of material. Here, we'll only cover the three main scenarios of non-implementation where a client / stakeholder:

- ...said they'd commit staff or budget, but doesn't;
- ...focused on the wrong things, e.g by devoting most attention and effort on low-reward areas;
- ...is unable to be certain or specific enough about ROI.

ROI UNCERTAINTY

The third of the three striking points is ROI.

29/51 (57%) of SEOs who responded to the survey felt a significant contributor to past non-implementation was the inability to be **certain enough** about ROI. Meanwhile 27/51 (53%) SEOs felt a significant contributor was an inability to be **specific enough** about ROI.

I hate being asked about the uplift for a granular component task. It's often an engagement flag, and it's often impossible to answer - like asking about the ROI of a daily shower on your future earning potential! With assumptions and conjecture, anyone can make up a credible answer.

But for SEOs, ROI ambiguity **hurts commitment**. Even if only tacitly. Our survey hinted towards this, but there's also academic evidence for it as "ambiguity aversion"[1].

Ambiguity aversion says we favour the known over the unknown, and prefer a poor chance of success over an unknown outcome.

In a classic experiment, participants were given two boxes of red and black balls, and told they'd win money for drawing a red ball. In one bag they knew the red/black mix was 50/50, in the other they had no idea. People tended to draw from the 50/50 bag - preferring a 50% chance of failure over a shot in the dark.

Plus, ambiguity actually amplifies a negative response to threat. In another study, participants were asked to touch uncomfortably hot plates. Those with less information about the plates felt pain more intensely [2].

Let's apply this to organic search, eg a site migration.

Migrations are risky if sloppy, take ages, inconvenience a number of different functions and can be tedious - particularly redirect mapping.

If mapping the last 20% of URLs will take much longer than the first 80%, expect to be asked about the impact of just redirecting them to the home page.

To get the right outcome, we have to resist ambiguity and uncertainty, and amplify what is certain to dial down a stakeholder's sense of threat.

Solution: amplify what is certain

We can use simple statements like:

- If designing the project from scratch, we would **definitely** do it like this.
- If we do it like this, our goal is **impossible / unlikely / possible / likely / highly likely.**
- If we do it differently, our goal is **impossible / unlikely / possible / likely / highly likely.**

These can cover topics like future: time, effort, money and other benefits. At Blue Array, we reiterate the eye-watering size-of-prize.

Positive tactics are always preferred for ROI uncertainty. They breed confidence, purpose, and energy. A study showed that students primed with positive attributes perform better **and** learn more from mistakes [3].

Conversely, picture someone who objects to everything, doesn't adopt a problem-solving mentality, and puts their energy into listing reasons a project will fail.

They can be effective at getting their way, but nobody likes them.

But if all else fails, we can use negativity to stop ROI-related non-implementation.

Solution: negative frames if needed

People are more willing to take risks to avoid losses than to make gains, and they feel losses twice as keenly than gains.

One experiment showed that employees given a bonus with the threat of revoking it put in more effort than those who received a bonus at the end of the year [4].

Let's apply this to a context for us.

We've all seen sites commit cardinal sins, but perform OK. Picture a site with doorway-esque conversion pages. While not successful, there could be no direct evidence they're problematic. You might **feel** they're dampening performance, but when asked about uplift from addressing - you might have to say... possibly nothing.

You might be forced to talk about avoiding losses instead. A penalty-type frame can be more effective than a reward frame for avoiding ROI-related non-implementation.

Again, this needs to be used sparingly because it won't win raving fans who sing our praises to others.

Plus, SEO "issues" are more concrete than SEO "opportunities". I don't want a stakeholder to fix some undefined canonical tag 'issues', then wonder why the money isn't rolling in.

Actionable recap:

If you're experiencing non-implementation as a result of ROI uncertainty, make stakeholder eyes water with the size of the prize. Then dial down ambiguity by amplifying what **is** certain, eg 'this is how we would do it if we were starting from scratch', 'if we do it this way our goal is possible / likely / highly likely'.

If this doesn't work, changing the frame to avoid losses can be highly effective, but it's energy sapping, and won't create raving fans.

FOCUSING ON THE WRONG THINGS

33/51 (65%) of SEOs reported non-implementation where a significant contributing factor was a client or stakeholder focusing on the wrong things (eg devoting most attention and effort on low-reward areas).

It was the second most striking finding in the survey.

A focus on the wrong things indicates a lack of understanding. That's attributable to us.

The survey was particularly revealing here. Respondents experiencing this also reported that communication was the least of their worries. Of these, 18 identified as 'senior manager' or "higher".

What could account for this? How could a focus on the wrong areas **not** be a communication issue?

As I see it, either:

- we're deluded about our communication.
- we're guilty of strategic misrepresentation
- there are biases impacting stakeholder decisions.

Let's assume that communication is sound, and explore a scenario to understand the focus on low reward areas.

An SEO audit uncovered opportunities and graded them by importance. Content consolidation was the key strategic enabler, but our backlog also contained priorities to optimise specific meta descriptions and to address specific redirect chains.

We agreed to work on something else while the client/stakeholder consolidated content. Time went by, and it wasn't actioned. Why? The client/stakeholder was under pressure to deliver various initiatives, and they relied on flawed mental shortcuts for decisions.

First, our stakeholder looked at meta descriptions because the brand copy had been bothering them for some time.

They were influenced by confirmation bias - the tendency to give more weight to evidence that supports an existing belief. The result was a problematic focus away from the the most significant SEO enabler.

Next, redirect chains were addressed. Why?

We can look for two flawed shortcuts. First, availability bias. It was coined by Daniel Kahneman and Amos Tversky, and suggests we give more weight to easily recalled information.

Content consolidation is abstract, and details don't come to mind quickly. Redirect chains are concrete, and the details come to mind quickly and potently. Our stakeholder gives them weight, and sets aside the need to gather complete information.

The second flawed shortcut is more deliberate.

Ex-Googler Maile Ohye said SEO typically takes 4-12 months to show results. But actioning redirect chains is immediately measurable through load speed, which suits stakeholders under pressure to report progress.

But this prioritises the wrong thing. Over-emphasis on reporting reinforces another common & problematic human tendency called present bias. This describes our tendency to prefer instant gratification.

There's academic evidence that humans actually prefer the poorer of two goals if the poorer is close at hand [5,6]. For example, when given the choice of receiving £150 today or £160 in 4 weeks, people tend to choose £150 today. But when offered the same in 48 or 52 weeks, people tend to choose £160 in 52 weeks - despite the time difference being the same.

If it happens with money, why would it not happen in SEO?

The content consolidation example is fictitious to illustrate a point, but

should resonate if you've experienced non-implementation because of focus on the wrong things.

There's a simple action to address this.

Solution: stop enabling distractions

Those reporting issues with stakeholder focus didn't report communication issues. Yet, we've enabled distractions by communicating actionable details on a spread of areas at once.

Why do we do this? To encourage simultaneous implementation from different groups? To delight stakeholders? Or as a spread bet in case a big ticket initiative isn't effective? Probably a mixture, but if it's distracting, it's wrong.

The simple action is to withhold actionable tactical details for lower priority tasks until big ticket ones are live.

Actionable recap:

Clear and rational communication isn't enough to stop a focus on low reward areas. We SEOs are accountable for bad focus by enabling too much choice. Let's withhold actionable details for smaller tasks until big ticket activites are live.

WITHHELD RESOURCES (STAFF OR BUDGET)

By some margin, the biggest reported issue was stakeholders saying they'd commit staff or budget, but then don't do it.

Remember, we specify the resources needed for SEO success. A stakeholder may U-turn for many legitimate reasons. But they're also at the mercy of optimism bias.

If you get frustrated that, while successful, your personal or professional projects rarely turn out exactly as envisaged, that's not you - that's just people.

Optimism bias dictates we're much more optimistic than realistic.

Humans tend to:

- overestimate our ability to control things;
- underestimate the control of others;
- often completely fail to acknowledge that what benefits us can also benefit others.

This is a big one. One study showed 80% of people rated themselves as above-average drivers [7], other work showed that people were way too optimistic about not being in a car accident [8], getting fired, or getting seriously ill.

SEO is so cross-functional that it's not surprising we're prone to this. A complete SEO is equally fluid and influential with developers, content, PR, and probably Marketing - often the budget that sponsors us.

Really, it follows that our stakeholders are susceptible to overestimating influence, and underestimating the control others have.

How do we offset this optimism bias to reduce non-implementation? The answer is... management!

Solution: stakeholder collaboration and emotional commitment

In the survey, those reporting a **collaborative** plan with specific outputs suffered much less from withheld resources. While withheld resources were the most problematic issue by some distance, this subset of respondents reported four or five more striking issues.

Why could this be? A tangible and collaborative plan reduces the likelihood of misunderstanding, or a disparity of understanding. It forces stakeholders to picture specific needs. The more collaboration and specificity early on, the higher the chances are that our clients and stakeholders will have access to the right resource.

It also allows us to leverage another, less rational tactic.

You may have heard of commitment or sunk cost bias? If you've ever pushed a doomed project through to completion, you've lived it. The same motivations that compel us to push on with doomed projects can be channeled to ignite projects that never got started due to lack of resources.

We are much more likely to see something through once we've made a small (but public and personal) commitment. It's why people run marathons despite being unfit, unwell or injured.

There's academic evidence too. A study found people who specified exercise goals and signed a token 'contract' were 50% more successful at hitting those goals than those without one [9].

Failure to deliver is a negative trait, so it feels better to not start a project than to start one you fear you'll fail. Of course agility is essential too; always pivot on a roadmap if circumstances change, but a collaborative and signed-off roadmap is an essential pre-commitment device for staving off procrastination or de-prioritisation.

Actionable recap:

Have stakeholders make a small emotional investment by collaborating on your roadmap (and personally signing off on some more realisable details). This small and frictionless commitment will massively increase their chances of understanding and supplying resources required.

IN SUMMARY

Finding #1

ROI uncertainty hampers implementation.

Actions

Dial down ROI ambiguity by amplifying what is certain.

If other options have been exhausted, respond to ROI questions with negative frames, but do so sparingly. Constantly flagging issues isn't exciting or energising, and won't turn stakeholders into raving fans.

Finding #2

Focusing on the wrong thing also hampers progress. Humans are prone to focussing on topics that come to mind easily, support an existing belief, and have a quick benefit.

Actions

Drip-feed actionable information for better stakeholder concentration and choices. Clear and rational communication won't prevent biases from affecting prioritisation.

Finding #3

Stakeholders often withhold the resources promised. This is not unusual or unique to SEO. ~80% of people are prone to overestimating their control and underestimating that of others.

Actions

Trigger emotional investment and personal commitment with a roadmap/plan that's collaborative, specific, and gets signed off by stakeholders.

Setting out requirements in advance is not enough.

SOURCES

[1] Ellseberg, D. (1961). Risk, Ambiguity, and the Savage Axioms. Quarterly Journal of Economics, 75 (4) 643–669

[2] Webb, C. (2018). Nudge thyself. Retrieved from Ogilvy Consulting UK YouTube channel

[3] Bengtsson, Sara & Dolan, Raymond & Passingham, Richard. (2011). Priming for self-esteem influences the monitoring of one's own performance. Social cognitive and affective neuroscience. 6. 417-25. 10.1093/scan/nsq048.

[4] Gächter, S., Orzen, H., Renner, E., & Starmer, C. (2009). Are experimental economists prone to framing effects? A natural field experiment. Journal of Economic Behavior & Organization, 70, 443-446.

[5] Ainslie, G. (2001) Breakdown of Will. New York, Cambridge University Press

[6] Ainslie, G. (1992). Studies in rationality and social change. Picoeconomics: The strategic interaction of successive motivational states within the person. Cambridge University Press.

[7] McCormick, I.A., Walkey;, F.H., Green, D.E. (1986). Comparative Perceptions of Driver Ability: A Confirmation and Expansion. Accident Analysis & Prevention 18 (3): 205–208.

[8] DeJoy, D. M. (1987). The Optimism Bias and Traffic Safety. Proceedings of the Human Factors Society Annual Meeting, 31(7), 756–759. https://doi.org/10.1177/154193128703100714

[9] Goldhaber-Fiebert, J. D., Blumenkranz, E., & Garber, A. M. (2010). Committing to exercise: contract design for virtuous habit formation (No. w16624). National Bureau of Economic Research.

Survey link: https://forms.gle/ka8S8xjmqpWS66US7

ABOUT BLUE ARRAY

Part agency. Part consultancy. "Consulgency", if you will.

We're not a traditional SEO agency. From the day we launched in early 2015, we've been pioneering a unique hybrid of agency and consultancy. It's an approach that allows us to give our clients the individual attention they need, at the same time as using proven techniques and tools honed in-house in an agency environment.

It's how we give you what we like to call an 'unfair advantage' over your competition.

Never having taken investment, we have bootstrapped our way to 45 employees, multi-million pounds of turnover, and becoming the UK's largest specialist SEO agency in five years.

Clients include heycar, RAC, Funding Circle and many more.

Find out more about us at bluearray.co.uk

SIMON SCHNIEDERS
Founder and CEO